LINESMANSHIP

The Art Of Enhancing
A Referee's Performance

by

D.C. Emerson Mathurin

Forward by

Jack Austin Warner

President of CONCACAF

Reproduction of Laws VI and XI is with the courtesy of FIFA.
Moreover, the diagrams in Chapter 3 illustrating points in connection
with the Diagonal System of Control have been adapted from the
1993 edition of FIFA's **LAWS OF THE GAME AND
UNIVERSAL GUIDE FOR REFEREES.**

Photo Credits

Front cover photograph by Pedro Alverez
Photographs on pages 49-51, by Grant Couch
inclusive
Back Cover Photograph by Alexandra

Layout and Cover Design Kimberly N. Bender

Also by D.C. Emerson Mathurin

IN SEARCH OF FAIR PLAY
A PRIMER FOR INSTRUCTORS OF BEGINNING SOCCER REFEREES
A SYLLABUS FOR THE CLASS 2 REFEREES' UPGRADING COURSE
A SYLLABUS FOR THE CLASS 1 REFEREES' UPGRADING COURSE

Co-author of:

PLAY ON - ADVANTAGE! THE BOOK OF SOCCER OFFICIATING
IN THE EYE OF THE WHISTLE: THE REFEREEING AT THE 1986 WORLD CUP
IN THE EYE OF THE WHISTLE: THE REFEREEING AT THE 1990 WORLD CUP

First Impression November 1995
Second Impression February 1998

© 1995 by D.C. Emerson Mathurin

Library of Congress Cataloging - in - Publication Data

Mathurin, D.C. Emerson
    Linesmanship

ISBN No. 1-890946-13-3
Copyright © 1998 D.C. Emerson Mathurin

Reedswain books are available at special discounts for bulk purchase. For details contact the Special Sales Manager at Reedswain 1-800-331-5191.

Published by **REEDSWAIN**
Books and Videos
612 Pughtown Road
Spring City, Pennsylvania 19475, USA
1-800-331-5191 • www.reedswain.com

To
Javier Arriaga Muñiz,
for all the right reasons.

The man who rows the boat
has no time to rock it!
Anon

Table of Contents

Foreword

Once again it does give me the greatest honor to write the foreword for a football publication - the fifth by FIFA Referee Instructor and Member of CONCACAF's Referees' Commission, D.C. Emerson Mathurin.

This book is a very useful guide for all practising linesmen, and it could not have been written at a more opportune time. Far too often we tend to concentrate on the "man in the middle", his strengths and weaknesses, his success or his failure in a particular match, as well as his deportment generally, and we pay too little attention to the men patrolling the touch-lines.

Good linesmen are as important for the efficient conduct of a match as are good referees, and it is my sincere hope that this book will contribute towards making our good linesmen better and linesmanship a career. I, therefore, recommend it as compulsory reading for every linesman and referee who wants to improve his career on the field of play.

Jack Austin Warner
President, CONCACAF

Preface

On December 12, 1991, Jack Warner, the President of CONCACAF (Confederation of North, Central American and Caribbean Association Football), wrote me a letter concerning one of my publications. He ended his missive by casually mentioning that he was awaiting my work with regard to linesmen. His casual statement turned out to be the seed of this book.

Since then, a number of developments have taken place in association football (or soccer, as most prefer to call it), not the least of which has been the establishment of a List of International Linesmen by FIFA (Fédération Internationale de Football Association), the international governing body of the sport. Indeed, the 3.6 million spectators who crowded stadia across the United States to watch the Final Tournament of the 1994 FIFA World Cup, and the billions of fans around the world who viewed the games on television, witnessed for the first time the use of specialist linesmen in this quadrennial competition.

Yet, as far as can be determined, and as unbelievable as it may seem, not a single textbook has ever been devoted exclusively to linesmanship, or to the art of running the line!

The work undertaken here is, therefore, pioneering, in the sense that one of the four objectives of this book is to fill the awesome gap in the literature on match officiating as it pertains to linesmanship.

The second objective of this work is to acquaint everyone with or to remind them of the very important role of linesmen as match officials, while the third objective is to provide instructors with reference material for training linesmen. Finally, this book has been written to provide national associations with criteria for measuring the efficiency of linesmen, and for measuring the abilities of their respective cadre of linesmen.

As a referee instructor, I have attempted to arrange the topics so that they follow a natural order. The discussion in Chapter 1 on the history of linesmanship and the Laws of the Game provides the setting for Chapter 2, in which an analysis of Law VI is undertaken. The analysis is centered around two very simple notions, namely, that a linesman shall be appointed to assist the referee to control the game in accordance with the Laws, and that, whereas linesmen opine, referees decide.

Chapter 2 also deals with aspects of referee-linesmen co-operation as a prelude to a relatively lengthy discussion in Chapter 3 on the Diagonal System of Match Control. Chapter 3 may be considered the heart of the book, dealing as it does with the movement and positioning of the referee and his linesmen, and the signals employed by them to communicate with each other.

Chapter 4 is devoted entirely to the Off-side Law, if only because the judgement of off-side is the most important task of a neutral linesman, whereas I use Chapter 5 to appeal to my fellow referees to fully appreciate the tremendous assistance that is provided to us by our linesmen, who, unquestionably, are our best friends on the field of play!

Chapter 6 outlines the criteria that I believe should be employed in assessing the strengths and weaknesses of a linesman in any particular match, and Chapter 7 contains a check-list that could be used by linesmen for post-game analysis. The work is rounded off in Chapter 8 with a description of practical drills for linesmen.

Now is probably the time for me to observe that, soon after I had completed my final manuscript, FIFA established and subsequently published a provisional List of International Women Referees and Lineswomen for 1995. Although I have used the term "linesman" throughout this book and the "he" of rhetorical convention when referring to the "linesman", I wish to emphasize that what I have written in the following pages is directed to lineswomen as well.

Writing a textbook of any kind is hard work. But the rewards could be great, and the greatest in this instance would be for the work to benefit some of the millions of linesmen who cheerfully carry out their duties to ensure the enhancement of referees' performances.

If the rewards for writing a book could be great, the acknowledgements for assistance received by the author could be even greater, as they are in this case. My first set of creditors are the hundreds of linesmen who, over the last thirty-three years, worked with me and always attempted to make me look good as a referee. You, and all the others I have watched, taught me most of what I know about linesmanship, and I earnestly thank you for that.

I owe a special debt to two colleagues, General Farouk Bouzo, Member of the FIFA Referees' Committee, and Osmond Downer, FIFA Referee Instructor, both of whom took the time to discuss linesmanship with me and to read the entire manuscript before it was submitted to the publishers. I am grateful for the stimulation of their insights and ideas, many of which are reflected in this book. My friend, Bill Hoyle, also read successive drafts of the book, and supplied me with eminently helpful suggestions, including those to improve both the clarity of the exposition and the style of writing. And, of course, I am thankful to Jack Warner for suggesting that I write this book.

None of the persons mentioned above should be blamed for the errors in this book. The responsibility for shortcomings is mine. Any credit, however, is due to my wife, Alexandra, to whom I express profound appreciation for gently prodding me to complete the book under very trying circumstances, and for relinquishing countless hours of my time that rightfully belonged to her. In four short years, she has learned so much about the game - the inside of it, the edge of it, and all around it!

D.C. Emerson Mathurin

The author with current FIFA President, Dr. João Havelange, at the CONCACAF Women's Championship in Montreal in August, 1994. It was under the auspices of Dr. Havenlange and during his tenure of office that FIFA established its International List of Linesmen and Lineswomen.

Author's Note To The Second Impression

At its annual meeting in Rio de Janeiro, Brazil, on March 9, 1996, the International Football Association Board decided to replace the words "linesman" and "Linesmen" in the Laws of the Game by the words "assistant referee" and "assistant referees." The Board reasoned that the old wording did not accurately reflect the task of a linesman who is, in actual fact, an assistant to the referee. Furthermore, the Board argued, the old wording did not reflect the fact that there are also women who provide assistance to referees.

Why, then, have I not used the new wording on this occasion?

It is precisely because this is a second impression, rather than a new edition of the work. By extension, I have not drawn on the Board's new (1997) revision of the text of the Laws of the Game. In any case, as pointed out by FIFA, the new revision has not changed the substance of the Laws, nor its Spirit.

The main reason, though, for my adherence to the wording in the first impression of this book is the fact that, no matter how one chooses to call the match officials who patrol the touch-lines, their task is still, by any other name, linemanship!

D. C. E. M.
July, 1997

GEN. FAROUK BOUZO

Hon. Treasurer : AFC
Chairman, Referees' Comm., AFC
Member, Referees' Comm., FIFA

Damascus - Syria
P.O. Box 34072
Tel : (Res) 963-11-4429360
Fax : (Res) 963-11-4420408

March 31, 1995

Mr. D.C. Emerson Mathurin
FIFA Referee Instructor
133 Shearer Crescent
Kanata, ON, Canada, K2L 3W2

Dear Mr. Mathurin:

It is with a great deal of interest and pleasure that I read your latest publication, **LINESMANSHIP: The Art Of Enhancing A Referee's Performance.**

I wish to congratulate you for your decision to undertake the work, and for the clear and detailed manner in which you have dealt with this most important aspect of match officiating. In particular, I am impressed by the way in which you have dealt with the role and responsibility of specialist linesmen in modern football, referee-linesman co-operation, the mental and physical preparation of linesmen, and the criteria that should be used in assessing the performance of a linesman.

Your work could not have been published at a better time. With FIFA's search for increased efficiency in linesman performance and for uniformity of linesmanship around the world, not to mention the obvious lack of reference material on the subject, there is no doubt that instructors will find the substance of your book of immense value. Indeed, referees and linesmen alike will benefit from studying the wealth of information in the book, which is why I expect all FIFA Confederations to approve its use for the training of referees, linesmen, instructors and assessors. Moreover, I expect and, in fact, hope that your efforts will encourage other experts to write on the subject under reference, thus filling the enormous void that exists in the literature on linesmanship.

Finally, I hope that as a result of your comprehensive treatment of the subject, everyone associated with our sport will come to fully appreciate the tremendous role and responsibility of the linesman.

Again, I congratulate you for writing yet another excellent book on an aspect of match officiating.

Yours sincerely,

General Farouk Bouzo
Member, Referees' Committee, FIFA

March 28, 1995

Mr. D.C. Emerson Mathurin
FIFA/CONCACAF Referee Instructor
133 Shearer Crescent
Kanata (Ontario)
K2L 3W2

Dear Emerson:

You have long worked and written on all aspects of refereeing in our game. As an important student and teacher of the game in Canada, you have devoted your energies to helping referees to better understand their role and refine their participation in the game. This book on linesmanship is another in a series of your writings for match officials and you have purposely referred to it in your subtitle as "The Art of Enhancing a Referee's Performance".

We are indeed a much stronger sport in Canada through your efforts. Although linesmen are rarely noticed until the crucial moment in a game, their role often makes the difference between a win and a loss. Over the past few years, the whole soccer community has recognized the need for proper training and high intensity opportunities for linesmen. The new FIFA initiative of creating a separate list for linesmen is a step in recognizing this most important aspect of the world premier sport.

Please accept my congratulations on your completion of yet another book on match officiating and my best wishes for succeeding in what you set out to do in undertaking the work. I am confident that your book will be a useful reference for our referees and linesmen, as well as for those who are responsible for training them.

Sincerely Yours,

Terry J. Quinn

1600 James Naismith Drive, Gloucester, Ontario K1B 5N4
Tel: (613) 748-5667   Fax: (613) 745-1938
Internet: bj895@freenet.carleton.ca

Affiliated to/Affiliée a la Fédération Internationale de Football Association

Prologue

Twenty-two years ago, in the autumn of 1972, I was appointed by The Canadian Soccer Association (CSA) to referee the Canadian Youth Championship Final between British Columbia and Quebec. The match was played on October 28 at the University of Montreal, on a soccer pitch atop a hill, amidst picturesque surroundings.

I was excited about the appointment for several reasons. In the first place, this was my third "plum" appointment in the middle in as many months, as I had already refereed the Ontario Cup Final in Toronto on August 20, and the Western Canada Cup Final in Vancouver on September 2. I vividly recall having excellent linesmen in both matches.

I was also excited, because these three matches came my way in less than ten months following my appointment as a National Referee by the CSA. Surely, I reckoned, with good assessments and the usual bit of good luck that every successful referee must have (like being in the right place at the right time), a nomination for my inclusion on FIFA's prestigious list of international referees could not be too far away!

There was also excitement within the CSA, for this was to be the first Youth Championship Final in the history of Canadian soccer. The plan, as explained to me then, was the selection of a national youth team by 1974, with the focus of the CSA being the 1976 Olympic Games in Montreal. Clearly, the top brass of Canadian soccer would be at the match, since many players on the field would likely form the nucleus of the team that would represent Canada in the XXI Olympiad. In fact, I knew that Dettmar Cramer, the famous FIFA coach from what was then West Germany, would be in attendance, for he was on a coaching assignment in Canada at the time. One single negative word from him about the officiating in the Youth Championship Final would likely be enough to dash any hopes I had of advancing my career as a referee.

And so I travelled to Montreal on the morning of the match, praying that I would be joined by two local linesmen who were capable of enhancing my field performance.

I need not have worried. My senior linesman, Les Pearson, was an experienced referee who was also a referee instructor. Significantly, there was something in the manner in which he spoke during our field inspection and in the silver flecks in his hair that told me he would give me maximum co-operation throughout the match.

My other linesman, Mike Bremer, was a small, dapper, young man with less than four years of refereeing experience. A seemingly phlegmatic sort, he exuded a quiet confidence as we changed into our uniforms and continued to refine the Third Team's game plan which we began discussing during inspection of the ground... linesmen to follow all moving balls to the goal-line; superfluous flag-waving to be avoided; eye contact to be maintained at all times, and especially before awarding a goal; acknowledgement of all signals by the linesmen; positions to be assumed by the officiating team at corner-kicks, penalty-kicks and free-kicks near goal . . .

Try as I may, I cannot remember the winner of the match. But it does not matter. What matters is my memory of the winning goal. More precisely, it is the manner in which that goal was scored, and the co-operation that I received from Mike Bremer in my decision to award it.

There was fierce action within the goal-area, to my right, and in full view of Bremer. Although I moved away from my diagonal and well into the penalty-area, I had difficulty in determining which players, attackers or defenders, were kicking the ball. Instinctively, I moved closer to the play, and glanced quickly at Bremer. There he was, standing near the corner-flagpost, on the balls of his feet, in the classic crouch of a linesman, flag held unfurled at his side and pointed towards the ground, his eyes focussed on the play. As I turned to the players, I lost sight of the ball momentarily. Now it was there, now it was not! Another quick glance at Bremer. Instantaneously, he raised his flag vertically and to its fullest extent. His eyes caught mine. We exchanged quick nods, confirming that the whole ball had crossed the goal-line, between the goal-posts and under the cross-bar. At the sound of my whistle, he lowered his flag, performed a pirouette that was worthy of Rudolph Nureyev, and, while maintaining eye contact with me, sprinted along the touch-line towards the half-way line. **GOAL**!

It was the first time in my twelve years of refereeing that I had not seen a ball enter the goal and had to depend upon my linesman to render an opinion before deciding to award a goal. By acting as decisively and correctly as he did, Mike Bremer simply enhanced my field performance as a referee on that day. He made me look good, very good, and thus began a friendship that has lasted for almost a quarter of a century.

It is my hope that this book will help in the development of the Mike Bremers who are constantly called upon to make referees look good!

D.C.E.M.
Ottawa, 1994

Chapter 1

Linesmanship and The Laws of the Game

An Historical Perspective

Historical evidence suggests that there was no need for match officials in the early days of the game of soccer. Players were expected to abide by whatever rules of play were in place, and any breach of the rules was assumed to have occurred either through inadvertence or ignorance of these rules. All disputes were quickly settled by the captains of the two teams. Thus, neither the referee nor the linesman was mentioned in 1862 by the Reverend J.C.Thring in his ten rules of what he called "The Simplest Game", or in the "Cambridge University Football Rules" that were published in October, 1863, or in the code of Laws that was framed by The Football Association out of the Cambridge Rules and was accepted on December 8, 1863.

By the time the FA Challenge Cup Competition was introduced in the season of 1871-72, it had become obvious to the FA that, with the increasing competitiveness of the game, players were intentionally infringing the rules of play. It became increasingly evident that not only was it necessary to impose penalties for breaches of the rules (especially those dealing with rough play), but also that there was need to have the game controlled by someone who was at once knowledgeable of the rules of play and neutral.

Two umpires and a referee were appointed by rival captains to matches in the Final Ties, that is, the semi-finals and the Final. Each half of the field of play was manned by an umpire who was equipped with a stick. The decision of the umpires was final, except in the case of disagreement between them when an appeal was made to the referee, whose decision was final. Whereas the umpires carried out their duties on the field of play, the referee was required to operate on the touch line, off the field of play.

The referee was first mentioned in the Laws in 1880 when his duties and powers were defined as follows:

"By mutual consent of the competing clubs in matches, a referee shall be appointed whose duty shall be to decide in all cases of dispute between its umpires. He shall also keep a record of the game and act as time-keeper

*and in the event of ungentlemanly behavior on the part of any of the
contestants, the offender or offenders shall, in the presence of the umpires, be
cautioned and in case of violent conduct, the referee shall have the power to
rule the offending player or players out of play and order him or them off the
ground, transmitting the name or names to the committee of the Association
under whose rules the game was played and in whom shall be solely vested
the right of accepting an apology."*

The referee was given additional power in 1890 when the International
Football Association Board, the "maker and keeper of the Laws" which was
formed in December, 1882. adopted a proposal that allowed him to stop play:

*". . .to award a free-kick, without any appeal, in any case where he thinks that
the conduct of a player is dangerous, or likely to prove dangerous. . ."*

No longer was the referee authorized to intervene only when the umpires
could not agree; he was now empowered in certain specific cases to interfere in
the game on his own initiative - but he was still kept off the field of play!

On June 2, 1891, the International Football Association Board effected several far-reaching changes to the Laws of the Game. Of particular interest was the
introduction of an entirely new law (Law 12) which placed the referee, complete
with whistle and notebook, instead of the umpires inside the playing area, and
which gave the referee autocratic powers in terms of match control. The new Law
12 is quoted below:

*"A referee shall be appointed, whose duties shall be to enforce the rules
and decide all disputed points. He shall also keep a record of the game
and act as time-keeper, and, in the event of any ungentlemanly behavior
on the part of any of the contestants, the offender or offenders shall be
cautioned, and, if the offence is repeated, or, in the case of violent
conduct, without any previous caution, the referee shall have the power
to rule the offending player or players out of play, and shall transmit the
name or names of such a player or players to his or their National)
Association, in whom shall be solely vested the right of accepting an
apology.*

*The referee shall have the power to terminate the game whenever by
reason of darkness, interference by spectators, or other cause, he shall
think fit, and he shall report the same to the Association under whose
jurisdiction the match was played, who shall have full power to deal with
the matter.*

Two linesmen shall be appointed, whose duty (subject to the decision of the referee) shall be to decide when the ball is out of play and which side is entitled to the corner-flag kick, goal-kick or throw-in. Any undue interference by a linesman shall be reported by the referee to the National Association to which the linesman belongs, who shall deal with the matter in such a manner as they may deem necessary.

The referee shall have the power to award a free-kick (without any appeal) in any case where he thinks the conduct of a player is dangerous or likely to prove dangerous, but not sufficiently so as to justify him in putting in force the greater powers vested in him as above."

In the context of linesmanship, two points need be made about the new Law 12. First, the term "umpires" was replaced by "linesmen" in the Laws of the Game. This is the first mention of linesmen in the Laws. The second point is that linesmen, now relegated to patrolling the touch-lines, were to have specific duties in assisting the referee with his control of the game. The linesmen were also required to carry flags in discharging their duties.

There is no indication in the new law whether linesmen were to be neutral, but this point must have been of concern to the authorities, for it was addressed by the Council of The Football Association in an 1895 publication of certain interpretations of the existing laws. The Council stated, inter alia, that

"In important matches it is desirable that linesmen should be neutral. Linesmen, where neutral, must call the attention of the referee to rough play or ungentlemanly conduct and generally assist him to carry out the game in a proper manner."

The importance of the Council's statement derives from the fact that it is the first time an indication is given of the co-operation that is essential between match officials in dealing with misconduct during a game.

The Referees' Association that was formed in 1893 followed up on the Council's statement. Included in 1896 in a special column called "Hints to Referees" in the very first issue of the Association's **REFEREES' CHART** is the advice that:

". . . the referee must be near the centre-line at the kick-off, in order to ensure that players did not encroach and that the ball moved forward. He must keep up with play and, when a goal was in question, see that the ball had actually passed beyond the goal-line.

"Linesmen should keep out of the field of play as much as possible, though close to the touchline. They should point with their flags to the spot where the ball went into touch, and stand on one side to watch the throw."

Al Pickford, a founding member of The Referees' Association, went further in describing the manner in which a referee and his linesmen should work together to control the game in the most efficient manner. Writing in his **ASSOCIATION FOOTBALL** in 1905, Pickford stated that:

"In practice the Linesman is entrusted with the oversight of the touch-line, he referee the goal-line and goal positions. This is a useful division of the work, but it is not a peremptory one - the linesman should keep an active watch on the ball crossing the goal-line so that he can if required help the referee either by signal or by consultation. The linesman should act as far as he can as a goal judge. To achieve this, the suggestion is made that one linesman should work more along the touchline on one half of the field of play and the other conversely."

The system described by Pickford is, in all likelihood, the genesis of the modern day Diagonal System of Match Control that was developed and employed by Sir Stanley Rous in the 1930s, and is now used almost everywhere in the world. The Diagonal System of Match Control is discussed in Chapter 3.

Sir Stanley Rous was also responsible for re-modeling the Laws of the Game into their present form. Until 1938, Laws 13 and 14 dealt with referees and linesmen, respectively. Since Sir Stanley's re-modeling in 1938, referees have been discussed in Law V, whereas Law VI has been devoted to linesmen.

Surprisingly, there has not been much change over the last fifty years in the text of the law that deals with linesmen. Indeed, the text of Law VI that appears in the 1995 edition of FIFA's **LAWS OF THE GAME** is almost identical in wording to the one issued in 1945, the main difference being the inclusion in the former of the duty of a linesman to indicate to the referee when a substitute is desired, and of International Board Decision 2 which states that in international "A" matches, national associations should appoint linesmen from FIFA's List of International Linesmen. The second inclusion became necessary with the establishment since 1992 of an official FIFA List of International Linesmen. The 1995 text of Law VI and its International Board Decisions are the subject of the next chapter.

Chapter 2

Law VI - Linesmen

"What has to be remembered is that no linesman ever gives a decision in any match. He can only indicate to the referee what his opinion is."

Denis Howell, **SOCCER REFEREEING**

Law VI

When the International Football Association Board held its annual meeting in FIFA House in Zurich, Switzerland on Saturday, March 5, 1994, it made a number of amendments to the Laws of the Game and to one of the existing International Board Decisions (IBDs). IBD 2 of Law VI was amended to reflect the fact that, since 1992, there has been an official FIFA List of International Linesmen. The complete text of Law VI, which deals with linesmen, and the IBDs related thereto is reproduced on the following page.

The first thing to be observed in Law VI is that linesmen shall be appointed by the authority under whose jurisdiction the game is to be played. In other words, the appointment of a linesman to a game is not a right to which he is entitled because he was successful in a referees' examination or because he is a member of a referees' association; rather, it is a privilege that has been extended to him to be part of a particular game. This view is supported by a directive in Law VI to the referee that he dispense with the services of a linesman who is guilty of undue interference or improper conduct. The law goes on to state that undue interference or improper conduct by a linesman shall be reported by the referee to the competent authority, because, in accordance with IBD 4 of Law VI, it is only upon a report of the referee that disciplinary action may be taken against a linesman for ". . . unjustified interference or insufficient assistance."

The second point to be noted is that Law VI states explicitly that a linesman shall assist the referee to control the game in accordance with the Laws. The operative word is assist, not insist, with the connotation that, whereas referees decide, linesmen opine. Thus, IBD 5 of Law V states that:

"Linesmen are assistants of the referee. In no case shall the referee consider the intervention of a linesman if he himself has seen the incident and from his position on the field, is better able to judge."

LAW VI - Linesmen

Two linesmen shall be appointed, whose duty (subject to the decision of the referee) shall be to indicate:

(a) when the ball is out of play,
(b) which side is entitled to a corner-kick, goal-kick, or throw-in,
(c) when a substitution is required.

They shall also assist the referee to control the game in accordance with the Laws. In the event of undue interference or improper conduct by a linesman, the referee shall dispense with his services and arrange for a substitute to be appointed. (The matter shall be reported by the referee to the competent authority.) The linesmen should be equipped with flags by the club on whose ground the match is played.

DECISIONS OF THE
INTERNATIONAL F.A. BOARD

(1) Linesmen, where neutral, shall draw the referee's attention to any breach of the Laws of the Game of which they become aware if they consider that the referee may not have seen it, but the referee shall always be the judge of the decision to be taken.

(2) In international "A" matches, national associations should appoint neutral linesmen from the International List.

(3) In international matches linesmen's flags shall be of a vivid colour, bright reds and yellows. Such flags are recommended for use in all other matches.

(4) A linesman may be subject to disciplinary action only upon a report of the referee for unjustified interference or insufficient assistance.

IBD 1 of Law VI reinforces the view that linesmen opine and referees decide in stating that:

"Linesmen, where neutral, shall draw the referee's attention to any breach of the Laws of the Game of which they become aware if they consider that the referee may not have seen it, but the referee shall always be the judge of the decision to be taken."

A third observation that can be made about Law VI is that it sets out the duties of a linesman in rather terse prose, although it is never altogether clear from the text whether the duties are those of a club or neutral linesman, or both. Indeed, notwithstanding the fact that probably more than half of the games played over the world are officiated by referees with club linesmen in support, nowhere in Law VI is the distinction clearly made between the two classes of linesmen. To be advised of the distinction, one has to refer to FIFA's memorandum on "Co-operation Between The Referee and Linesmen" in the 1995 edition of **LAWS OF THE GAME**. Therein, FIFA distinguishes, at least implicitly, the difference between club and neutral linesmen.

Club And Neutral Linesmen

As opposed to a neutral linesman who is a qualified referee, a club linesman is someone who has been pressed into action, often by a club, to signal to the referee when the ball has gone out of play beyond the touch-line or the goal-line. In the circumstances, club linesmen are sometimes asked by some referees to indicate which team should restart play, that is to say, whether a corner-kick or a goal-kick is to be awarded, or which side is entitled to the throw-in. It would appear, though, that most referees prefer asking club linesmen to do nothing more than signal when the ball has crossed a boundary line.

On the other hand, in addition to performing all the duties outlined for club linesmen, neutral linesmen are asked to perform a very important duty, namely, to assist the referee in conducting the game in accordance with the Laws.

How does a neutral linesmen perform this important duty? Typically, he does so by indicating off-side infractions to the referee, calling the attention of the referee to rough play or misconduct, indicating to the referee when a substitution is desired, and giving an opinion on any point on which the referee may consult him. These duties are clearly not the kind that a referee should entrust to club linesmen, many of whom may be substitutes or injured players, team officials, parents, and the like!

Regardless of their status, club and neutral linesmen are reminded by FIFA that ". . . (they) must, for their part, fully appreciate the referee's supreme authority and accept his rulings without question should there be any difference of opinion amongst them. They must be supportive and never contradict his decisions." To reinforce this reminder, the opening sentence of Law VI stipulates that the duty of a linesman is subject always to the decision of the referee.

Referee-Linesmen Co-operation

The remainder of this chapter deals with aspects of referee-linesmen co-operation as a prelude to the discussion on the Diagonal System of Match Control in the following chapter. The emphasis is on the co-operation between the referee and his neutral linesmen, although it is very important for a referee to also tell club linesmen before the start of a match how best they could assist him.

Where club linesmen are appointed to support a referee, they should be given clear instructions by him that their assistance shall be restricted to signalling when the ball goes out of play beyond the goal-line or touch-line, whether on the ground or in the air. The referee should stress to them in a calm and unofficious manner that the whole ball must be over the entire line before they signal that the ball is out of play. He should also inform them that, notwithstanding their personal opinion, his decision is final and is not to be questioned in any way - at least, not on the field of play!

Where neutral linesmen are appointed to assist the referee, it is the latter's responsibility to ensure that the match officials act as a team. At the higher levels of the game, referees and their linesmen often travel to game sites together. The smart referee uses such occasions to develop a rapport with his linesmen.

Often, he manages to do this by putting the shy ones at ease, sometimes by encouraging the taciturn ones to describe some of their game experiences, or by leading a discussion on the rules of the competition, or by talking about The Game in general. Sometimes, rapport can be developed by a simple "getting to know you" conversation between the three officials, during which they talk about themselves - their jobs, families, training methods, mutual friends, and the like.

If the referee knows nothing about the two teams, or if his knowledge of them is limited, he may turn to his linesmen to draw on any knowledge that they might have, and there and then begin to map out the Third Team's game plan. Does either team play a physical game? How physical? Do they both play that game? Are their players quick? If so, throughout the game, or simply at certain times, and within certain areas on the pitch? Do the players engage in gamesmanship? Who is the famous gamesman? What about "professional" fouls? Is either team an exponent of this sort of negative play? Is either team noted for indulging in "off-the-ball" incidents? Do the players on both teams tackle cleanly? Are any of them prone to playing "over the top" on the pretext of tackling for the ball? What about the off-side trap? Is the tactic exploited by either team? Are the coaches and other team officials reasonable men and women, or are they the type who would attempt to win games at any cost? What might we expect from the spectators?

The foregoing are some of the questions that a referee and his linesmen might have to consider as the referee maps out the game plan for the three of them.

Upon arrival at the park, the referee should continue developing rapport between him and his linesmen. It should begin with the inspection of the field and the appurtenances of the game, with the referee and linesmen (and the fourth official, if one is appointed) checking the field of play together to ensure that it is correctly marked with distinctive lines that are no more than five inches in width. The remainder of the check-list here includes a rectangular playing surface that poses no threat to the safety of players; goals, goal-areas, penalty-areas, penalty-kick marks, restraining arcs, corner-quadrants and a centre-circle of the dimensions that are laid down in Law I; and corner-flagposts that are not less than five feet high.

The foregoing is, of course, tantamount to a partial review of Law I, and, in the context of match control, must be taken as seriously as the other Laws of the Game by the referee and his linesmen, given that these laws are inextricably linked to each other. Furthermore, referees must realize that the assistance to be given to them by linesmen often begins with Law I. Yet, so many referees simply say "Check the nets" to inexperienced linesmen, without instructing the latter that they should ensure that nets, where provided, are securely attached to and appropriately supported by the goal-posts and cross-bar, will not be a hindrance to the goalkeeper, and are securely fastened to the ground. Moreover, linesmen should ensure that holes in the nets are not large enough to permit the ball to slip through, and they should be satisfied that the hooks to which the nets are attached pose no danger to players and match officials.

Frequently, it is during the inspection of the field that the referee informs his linesmen which diagonal he intends to use, and the side of the field which each linesman shall patrol in each half of the match. All of this points to one very good reason why match officials should be at the park long before the opening kick-off - at least half an hour before, and earlier if league requirements so dictate.

In the dressing room and, in any event, well before the match begins, the referee should co-operate with his linesmen on the following points.

- The time by his watch (the referee and his linesmen should synchronize their watches before the start of the match; the referee should decide which linesman will keep running time, and which one will be responsible for stop time)
- Who shall be the senior linesman, and who, therefore, shall be responsible for assisting him in controlling the team benches and ensuring that substitution during the game is effected in accordance with Paragraph 5 of Law III
- The duties of the linesmen prior to the start of the game and at half-time or extra time or deciding kicks from the penalty-mark (for

example, examining players' equipment, checking team colors, and reporting to the referee any irregularity with competition rules)
- Record-keeping (kick-off time, goals scored, team colors, players cautioned and dismissed, names of team captains and team officials, etc.)
- The mutual acknowledgement of signals
- All the technical aspects of game control, field coverage, positioning and signaling as described in the following chapter on the Diagonal System Match Control

Included under the last point are the following considerations:
- The referee should remind his linesmen that not only are they to watch the ball upfield, but how vitally important it also is for them to watch the players behind him and to bring off-the-ball incidents to his attention.
- The referee should remind his linesmen that, when he is engaged in attending an injury or administering discipline to a player, the linesman nearest the place of stoppage should move to a position in line with that place; if possible, the linesman should try to secure the ball, and, if asked, he should be able to advise the referee what the restart should be, and by whom the ball should be put in play.

Where the referee leaves the dressing room without covering all or even any of the points outlined above during his pre-game instructions to his linesmen, a linesman should never hesitate to ask the referee how best he could assist him in conducting the game in accordance with the laws. And whereas linesmen are trained to be **assistants** rather than **insistants** (there may be no such word, but there certainly is such a condition!), they should literally force the referee's hands on those occasions by asking him such questions as:

- What assistance would you like me to give you in dealing with player misconduct that may have escaped your attention?
- Where would you like me to position myself at corner-kicks, goal-kicks, free-kicks, penalty-kicks, etc?
- What duties should I perform when a penalty-kick is being taken?
- Would you like me to signal for infringements, and especially those that occur near to me or out of your view? In the circumstances, what signals would you like me to use?
- How long would you like me to maintain my off-side signals?
- What, if any, time signals would you like me to give you?
- Are there any "silent" signals that you will be giving me and the other linesman, or any that you will wish me to use on particular occasions?
- What assistance would you like me to give to you at substitutions?

- Do you have any special instructions for me with regard to control of the team benches?
- At throw-ins, who will be responsible for each of hand and foot faults?
- How are you going to acknowledge that you have seen my signal, but that you are overruling me?
- Would you like me to join you at centre-field for the coin toss?

It was mentioned earlier that referees often use travel time to exchange information with their linesmen about a particular match. For the majority of matches, however, referees and linesmen travel independently to grounds, and this exchange of information takes place in the dressing room, usually during the referee's pre-game instructions.

Before leaving the dressing room, the referee should make a final check to ensure that all three match officials are fully equipped for the match - two watches (one with stop action), notebook or scorecard, pencils, coins, whistles, disciplinary cards, and, in the case of the linesmen, flags. Why should the linesmen carry these "tools of the trade"? It is because they may be called upon to take over the match without warning, for example, in the event the referee becomes incapacitated.

The referee should, of course, leave the dressing room with the game ball, although it is becoming more common for each linesman also to carry a spare ball as the Third Team moves to the centre-circle. At the higher levels of the game, it is the fourth official who is given the spare balls for safekeeping. Finally, before the kick-off, the linesmen should check the goal nets once more to make certain that everything is in order.

In CONCACAF, linesmen are advised to keep their flags furled as they enter the field of play with the referee prior to the start of a half, and, after assuming the appropriate position on the touch-line, to unfurl the flags as a signal to the referee that they (the linesmen) are ready for the start of play.

So far, much of the emphasis has been placed on the role of the referee in ensuring that the game plan of the match of officials is mapped out, and that the match officials act as a team. It is obvious, however, that the more a linesman knows about the qualities of a referee, the better he is able to assist him in establishing and maintaining match control. It is this knowledge that almost invariably helps a linesman to detect that something is amiss with a referee's performance, and causes him, without being unnecessarily intrusive, to take whatever action is necessary to enhance that performance.

Before the end of the first half of play, and under normal circumstances, the observant linesman should have answers to most, if not all of the following questions about the referee:

- How has he controlled play?
- How has he controlled the game?
- Has he been in control of himself?
- How has he exercised the authority and the sweeping powers granted to him in the Laws of the Game?
- Is he respected by the players and the team officials?
- How effective has he been in communicating with the players and his linesmen?
- Has he been impartial?
- Has he demonstrated that he is match-fit?
- How has he positioned himself in static and dynamic situations?
- Has he demonstrated a capability for interpreting both the Letter and the Spirit of the Law correctly?
- Has he been using common sense in his refereeing?

At the half-time signal, the two linesmen, with flags furled, should join the referee so that they may leave the field of play together, after the players. This is obviously not the time for animated conversation nor for any gesture which would suggest to players and spectators that there had been disagreement between the match officials during the half. Neither is it the time for any of the match officials to stop on the way to the dressing room to chat with players and spectators. Instead, the officials should go straight to their dressing room, for there is work for them to do within.

Once in the privacy of the dressing room (and I am of the strong opinion that, unless by invitation of the referee, assessors and match commissaries have no business in there at this time!), it is the referee's responsibility to ensure that the half-time interval is well spent. Many referees, and especially the humble ones who appreciate that no one is perfect (". . . the perfect referee has yet to be born, and his father died years ago!"), set the tone by asking their linesmen a very simple question: What did I miss? Following discussion of any deficiency, real or imagined, in his officiating during the half, the referee should proceed in a very constructive manner to point out to each linesman, if appropriate, how referee-linesman co-operation could be improved in the second half.

The half-time interval in their dressing room is not an occasion for accusatory finger-pointing. Instead, the referee should take the lead role in discussions aimed at ensuring that, through their field performances, match officials will help in creating an atmosphere in which all players will observe both the Letter and the Spirit of the Law throughout the second half. Incidentally, it is not unusual to see an experienced linesman assist a young referee to assume this leadership role.

Typically, the end of half-time discussions between the referee and his linesmen revolve around a very simple, but important theme: What can we expect in the second half? Perhaps a change of tactics to more robust tackles as Reds press for the equalizer. Difficulty in controlling the team benches. Blues are likely to continue playing the "off-side trap". Blues are likely to indulge in gamesmanship in general and time-wasting tactics in particular as they protect their one-goal lead. Spectators may be very noisy, and it may be very difficult to hear the whistle. This is clearly a time for the referee and the linesmen to be very honest with each other, and for linesmen to be willing to share fully with the referee what, in the context of match control, they have perceived to be tendencies of certain players. After all, isn't match control everything that a referee does to prevent a game from falling into disrepute?

After a final check that all is well (linesmen should make certain that the referee does not forget the game ball in the dressing room, and the referee should ensure the linesmen, in turn, do not leave their flags in there, either!), the match officials should again enter the field of play together, as a team. Subsequently, the linesmen should break out and inspect the goal nets prior to the kick-off.

Post-game activities in the dressing room should include a comparison of notes by the referee and the linesmen, completion of necessary paperwork, and a discussion based again on a very simple question posed by each official: What did I miss?

Chapter 3

The Diagonal System of Match Control

Introduction

There are several systems of match control in current use. The system used at any particular time depends greatly upon whether the referee is officiating alone, whether he has only one linesman (and a club linesman at that!), whether he has two club linesmen assisting him, or whether he is being supported by two neutral linesmen. Stanley Lover has pointed out in his **ASSOCIATION FOOTBALL MATCH CONTROL** that, depending on the circumstances described above, a referee may employ the straight line patrol, the zig-zag patrol, the oval patrol, or even a combination of these three patrols in his coverage of the field of play.

Undoubtedly, the system most commonly used all over the world is the Diagonal System of Match Control, hereinafter also referred to as the Diagonal System of Control or the Diagonal System. The system was first introduced by the late Sir Stanley Rous when he refereed the FA Cup Final of 1934 at Wembley, and was subsequently approved by the International Football Association Board. It is the system used by referees when their linesmen are neutral.

This chapter is devoted to the Diagonal System of Match Control. The subject is treated under two headings, namely, movement and positioning of the referee and his linesmen, and the signals employed by the referee and his linesmen to communicate with each other.

MOVEMENT AND POSITIONING

The Diagonal System Of Match Control Defined

Simply stated, the Diagonal System of Match Control is a tactical method of control whereby two officials (the referee and one linesman) are present at all times in the attacking or "danger" zone with the play between them, and with the second linesman positioned in a way to assist the referee in the event of a quick counter-attack.

This is illustrated in Diagram 1 in which the referee patrols diagonally across

Diagram 1

DIAGONAL SYSTEM OF CONTROL

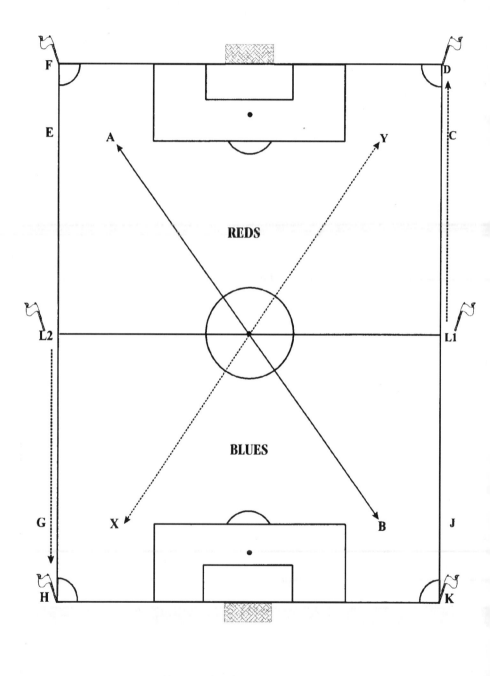

The author discussing the Laws of the Game with former FIFA President Sir Stanley Rous, at a banquet in Toronto in April 1979. As a referee, Sir Stanley invented the Diagonal System of Match Control in the 1930s, and he is the person responsible for the codification of the Laws of the Game as we know them.

the field of play along an imaginary line, AB, while each linesman supervises one-half of the field by patrolling the touch-line to that half.

In the diagram, Linesman L1 adopts the BLUES as his side, with Linesman L2 adopting the REDS. When the referee is up with the play at A, Linesman L1 should be at a point between C and D. As the play moves towards the other half, Linesman L1 moves so as to be positioned in line with the second last defender, a position that is referred to throughout this chapter, and is discussed in greater detail in Chapter 4 which deals with Law XI: Off-side. For now, suffice it to say that, in practice, rarely will Linesman L1 get into BLUES' half of the field. When the referee is at B, Linesman L2 should be somewhere between G and H. Again, it is rare that Linesman L2 will get into REDS' half of the field.

In the situation described above, the referee is said to be "taking the left wingers." Sometimes, however, a referee will use the opposite diagonal, that is, XY, in which case he would be "taking the right wingers." His linesmen would adjust accordingly, if only to maintain the principle of the Diagonal System of Match Control, that is, having the referee and a linesman together in the attacking zone, with the ball between them.

LINESMANSHIP

Clearly, the Diagonal System is likely to fail if the referee and a linesman find themselves in the same place at the same time, performing the same task. This will be so if, for example, Linesman L1 finds himself between J and K when the referee is at B, or if Linesman L2 is anywhere near E or F when the referee is at A. Other situations that are likely to result in a breakdown of the Diagonal System are described in the summary and conclusions at the end of this chapter.

It is generally agreed that the Diagonal System is the most efficient technique yet devised for optimum field coverage by the three match officials, and that the success of.the system is largely dependent upon two factors, namely,

- movement and positioning of the referee and the two linesmen
- co-operation between the three, that is, communication by the referee to the linesmen and, reciprocally, by the linesmen to the referee

Let us take a more detailed look at the referee and his linesmen during the game.

Basic Positions

Anyone who watches the movements of a competent referee in dynamic situations, that is, while the ball is in play, quickly realizes that they are not confined to positions along an imaginary straight line (for example, AB or XY in Diagram 1). Instead, the movements take place within a large Figure 8, or along a large letter S, or, more commonly, along a series of Zs that are joined together at their tails. Such movements allow the referee to:

- avoid interfering with play
- assume positions where his presence is needed
- cut down on travelling distances in crises (the shortest distance between two points remains a straight line!)

On the other hand, since his most important task is to cover off-side (and yet Law VI makes no reference to it!), a linesman's basic position is in line with the second last defender (or the last two defenders, if they are level with each other) or the ball or the attacker with the ball, whoever or whichever is nearest to the defenders' goal-line. From this position, the linesman is able to judge off-side or whether the ball has gone out of play over the goal-line for a goal-kick or a goal, or for a corner-kick. This explains why linesmen should follow all moving balls to the goal-line. Why is it sometimes necessary for the linesman to stay in line with the ball or the attacker with the ball? It is because a player can never be off-side if he is not in front of the ball or if he is not nearer to the opponents' goal-line than at least two of his opponents (See Paragraph 1 of Law XI).

With these basic positions out of the way, let us describe the positions of the referee and the linesmen in static situations, that is, at kick-offs, goal-kicks, corner-kicks, free-kicks, penalty-kicks and throw-ins, bearing in mind that all positions taken by the linesmen during a game should be the result of explicit instructions from the referee.

Kick-off

Let us assume, as in Diagram 2, that the kick-off is in direction BA. The referee should be at R, next to the defending forwards, and in a position where he can easily detect encroachment by players on either team.

Since, at a kick-off, the attackers almost invariably kick the ball backwards once it is in play, it seems wise for the referee to position himself at kick-offs next to the defending forwards where there is little chance of him interfering with play. FIFA's recommended position for the referee at kick-offs is slightly different in that it is suggested he stand in the attackers' half, again outside the centre-circle, but directly opposite to the position shown in Diagram 2. It is easier, though, for the referee to interfere with play if, at kick-offs, he assumes the position that is recommended by FIFA.

As to the linesmen, they will position themselves as illustrated in Diagram 2, that is, in line with the second last defender. This is in accord with FIFA's recommendation. Some referees instruct their linesmen to stand near the halfway-line at kick-offs, perhaps believing that the presence of the linesmen will deter players from entering into the opponents' half before the ball is kicked. The evidence suggests, though, that encroachment at kick-offs takes place mostly in and around the centre-circle. To the extent that this is true, the referee should be able to see the infringement quite clearly and deal with offenders firmly, especially where the offenders' act is blatant. In the circumstances, the referee could as well instruct his linesmen to stand in line with the second last defender at kick-offs so that they might be able to assist him in the event of very quick counter-attacks.

There is yet another possible advantage in having the linesmen at the halfway-line at kick offs. Where the referee prefers the "wrong" diagonal (that is, he takes the right wingers), it helps to remove the confusion and doubt of the linesmen if, immediately after the kick-off, they must run north or south (or east or west, depending on the location of the field of play) along the touch-lines and into their diagonal positions on the on-side/off-side lines. It also triggers activity and brings the linesman into play. Thereafter, it is easier for each linesman to remember what part of the touch-line he is to patrol.

Other referees instruct their linesmen to stand midway between the half-way line and the second last defender at kick-offs. Effectively, the linesmen are placed in a "no man's land" where it is virtually impossible for the referee to make the most efficient use of them.

Diagram 2

DIAGONAL SYSTEM OF CONTROL
KICK-OFF

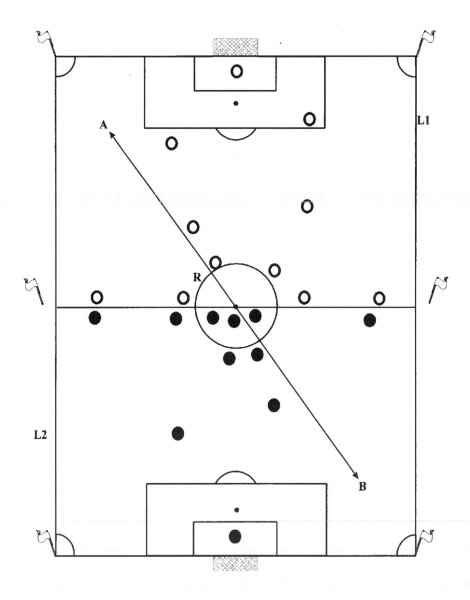

Goal-kick

As soon as a goal-kick has been awarded, the linesman will move along the touch-line until he is level with the goal-area line that is parallel to the goal-line, that is, to the 6-yard line. From that position, he can determine whether the ball is properly placed within the goal area, and especially that part of the area closest to him. (Remember that at the taking of a goal-kick, the ball may be placed anywhere within the goal-area).

Once he is satisfied that the ball is properly placed for the goal-kick, the linesman will move quickly to the forward edge of the penalty-area, that is, to the 18-yard line. There, he should ensure that the ball is in play (that is, it is kicked beyond the penalty-area) before it is touched or played by a second player. These movements by the linesman are illustrated in Diagram 3. With the linesman positioned at the edge of the penalty-area for the goal-kick, he will need to be very quick on his feet to assume the appropriate position to judge off-side in the event of a counter-attack.

At a goal-kick, the referee should stand around midfield and, in any event, adjacent to where the ball is expected to land so that he may have a full view of the players who will be challenging for the ball. Should he stand at R as in Diagram 3, he would have Linesman L1 in full view, and, with a slight twist of the body, Linesman L2 as well. He would also be in a position to make judgements involving both the goal-area and penalty-area lines that are parallel to the touch-line and away from Linesman L1.

Corner-kick

FIFA's recommendations to referees and linesmen is that, at a corner-kick, the officials are to position themselves as indicated in Diagram 4, ". . . no matter at which corner-area the kick is taken." In the positions indicated, the referee (R) moves away from his diagonal and travels towards the goal-area along the dotted line, as necessary; Linesman L1 stands behind the corner-flagpost, out of the kicker's way, or along the goal-line, approximately 11 yards from the corner-flagpost, and Linesman L2 stands at or near the halfway-line, poised to assist the referee in the event of a clearance or a counter-attack by the defending team.

From his position along the dotted line, the referee is able to detect goal-mouth scrimmages and infractions within the penalty-area, and to judge off-side immediately following the corner-kick. (Remember that, according to Paragraph 3(b) of Law XI, a player shall not be declared off-side if he receives the ball direct from a corner-kick).

With Linesman Ll standing behind the corner-flagpost, he is positioned to:
  • observe whether the ball is correctly placed within the corner-
    quadrant (as shown in the inset of Diagram 4)

- view incidents that may have escaped the referee
- determine whether the ball is in or out of play over the goal-line (that is, he acts as a goal judge)
- assist the referee in some cases in judging off-side situations.

A big advantage in having Linesman L1 stand along the goal-line is that, from this position, it is easy for him to assist the referee in dealing with defenders who encroach within 10 yards of the ball, a situation that is likely to occur on short corner-kicks. This distance is readily determined where there is the optional mark that may be drawn off the field of play, 11 yards from the corner-flagpost and at right angles (but not touching) the goal-line. The mark is, of course, 10 yards from the place where the quarter-circle meets the goal-line.

One disadvantage of having Linesman L1 on the goal-line at a corner-kick is that it is very difficult, if not impossible at times, for him to determine from that position whether the ball travelling over his head is in or out of play. Indeed, the nearer he is to the goal-post, the more difficult it may be for him to make that determination.

Yet another disadvantage of having Linesman L1 on the goal-line at corner-kicks is that he can rarely assist the referee in judging off-side infractions until he (Linesman L1) has regained his position on the touch-line. It is true that, in the circumstances, the referee should cover off-sides for the linesman, and that he should continue to do so until the linesman assumes the appropriate position. It is equally true, though, that the referee would be left far behind the play should there be a quick clearance from the corner-kick.

The movements of the referee and his linesmen at a counter-attack following a corner-kick are typically those depicted in Diagram 5. Linesman L2 moves towards the goal-line as play develops, positioning himself in line with the second last defender and in such a way to see infringements clearly until the referee catches up with play. These movements by Linesman L2 also ensure that there is at least one match official always up with play.

At the same time, and bearing in mind that the shortest distance between two points is a straight line, the referee sprints along the dotted line to regain his position on the diagonal, near play. Referees who can pass the FIFA's physical fitness tests at any time during the playing season are able to do so easily. For his part, Linesman L1 hurries back to his basic position on the touch-line, watching at the same time for off-the-ball incidents that may have to be brought to the referee's attention.

Diagram 3

DIAGONAL SYSTEM OF CONTROL
GOAL-KICK

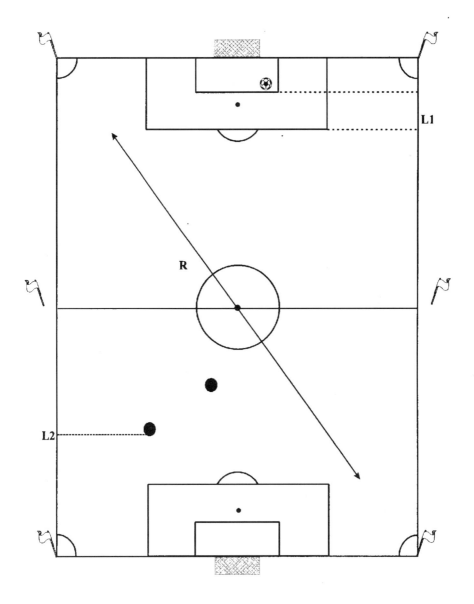

Diagram 4

DIAGONAL SYSTEM OF CONTROL
CORNER-KICK

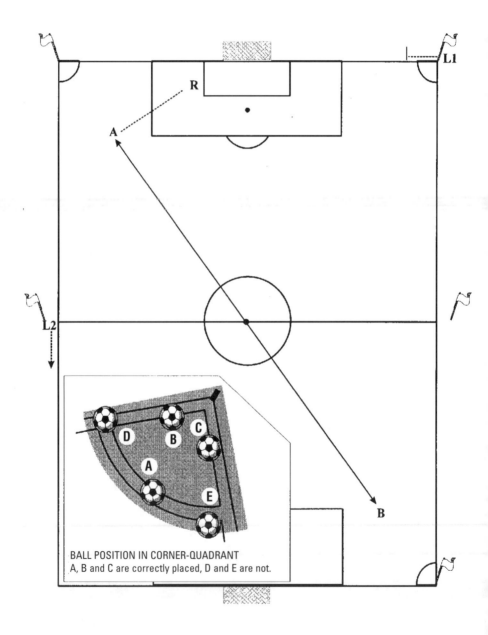

BALL POSITION IN CORNER-QUADRANT
A, B and C are correctly placed, D and E are not.

Diagram 5

DIAGONAL SYSTEM OF CONTROL
A COUNTER-ATTACK

(following a corner-kick)

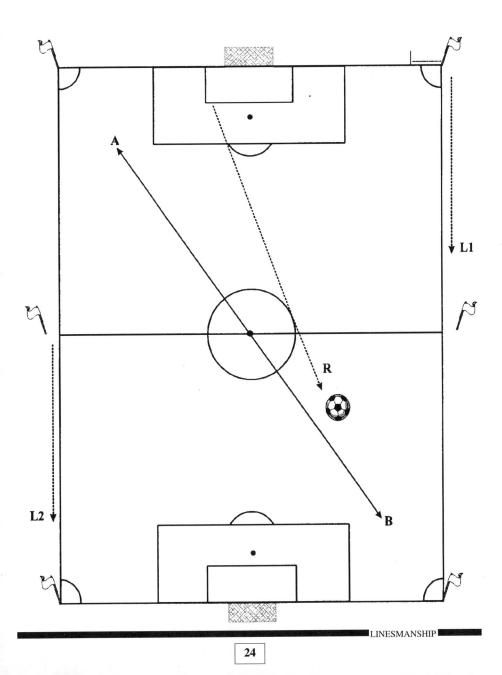

Free-kicks

The movement and positioning of the referee and his linesmen for free-kicks depend on whether the kick is to be taken at midfield or close to goal. In either case, however, it is important for the referee to adopt techniques that will facilitate the taking of quick free-kicks by the non-offending team, and discourage the offending team from indulging in tactics that are likely to result in so-called "ceremonial" free-kicks.

(a) Free-kicks In Midfield

Where the free-kick is at midfield, as in Diagram 6a, the system of movement and positioning adopted by the referee for himself and his linesmen is relatively straightforward. The referee should generally position himself on his diagonal near the area of play, that is, where the kick is expected to land, since this is the place where the players will be challenging for the ball. From this position, the referee can observe infringements, although his mere presence near the players may deter them from infringing the Laws of the Game. He may even be able to judge off-side infractions, depending on how close he is to the on side/off-side line. And, of course, he is in position to sprint to catch up with play should there be a clearance of the ball by the defenders.

Linesman L1 assumes his basic position to judge off-side, and he is able to move along the touch-line towards the corner-flagpost if play proceeds towards goal. Linesman L2 positions himself in line with the kicker, mainly to see that the ball is correctly placed and, as instructed by the referee, that the other requirements of Law XIII are met. Linesman L2 must also be prepared to assist the referee in case of a counter-attack.

(b) Free-kicks Near Goal

When the free-kick is outside the penalty-area but near goal, as in Diagram 6b, supervision of the play by the match officials becomes more critical, and certainly more demanding. First of all, one of the of officials has to be on the goal-line, acting as a goal judge should there be a direct hard shot on goal. Some referees prefer to assume that role, leaving the linesman in the attacking zone to take the line of defenders. The obvious problem with this division of labor is that the linesman is left to deal with match control problems at the line, even though he may well be 50 yards or so from would-be offenders. From this distance, it is virtually impossible for him to deal with the usual grabbing and pushing that takes place at the line.

Most referees prefer to adopt the movement and positioning that have been recommended by FIFA for free-kicks near goal, first, by taking the line of defenders themselves, and, second, by positioning the linesman in the attacking zone on the goal-line. (As an aside, it must be emphasized that the referee has sole responsibility for sending the linesman to the goal-line, and that the linesman should never move into that position until he has received a clear signal from the referee to do so; moreover, when sending the linesman to the the goal line, the referee should not signal for the free-kick to be taken until the linesman has reached the corner-flagpost). The referee thus judges off-side infractions himself, and is able to deal promptly with misconduct at the "wall".

Such dealings by the referee are often his "moments of truth", and it certainly helps if he is already at the scene of the crime when he has to administer the Laws of the Game. Of course, the referee who takes the line of defenders himself is also better positioned to catch up with play in the event of a long clearance by the defending team.

Penalty-kick

The positions to be assumed by the referee and his linesmen at a penalty-kick are illustrated in Diagram 7. As soon as a penalty-kick is awarded, Linesman Ll moves, first, along the touch-line and then the goal-line, and he positions himself at the intersection of the goal-line and the penalty-area line. From this position, Linesman L1 performs two specific duties: (a) he watches the goalkeeper to see that, in accordance with Law XIV, he is standing on his own goal-line, between the goal-posts; and (b) he acts as a goal judge.

With Linesman L1 responsible for performing these duties, this permits the referee to concentrate on all the other aspects that make Law XIV the veritable minefield that it is. Aside from overseeing the kick, the referee has to be on the look-out for possible infringements (e.g., misconduct) that are unrelated to Law XIV. He also has to observe infringements by the kicker, the goalkeeper, and their respective teammates. In the circumstances, FIFA once recommended that the referee stand at R, as in Diagram 7, and most referees seemed to favor that position. However, with the 1995 rewording of Law XIV and the requirement that, at a penalty-kick, all players with the exception of the kicker and the opposing goal-keeper must stand behind the penalty-mark, R1 is clearly an excellent place for the referee to stand. Should the referee be concerned with the activities of players who might be standing behind him at a penalty-kick, another excellent position for him to assume in the circumstances would be just outside the penalty-area, next to R1, but still in line with the penalty-mark.

It has been observed, though, that some referees stand within the goal-area at penalty-kicks. This is not advisable, since the ball could easily strike them or rebound from a goal-post and subsequently from them, and into goal ! A minority of referees choose to stand on the goal line, between the intersections of the goal-area and penalty-area lines and the goal-line. This, too, does not appear to be a good position for the referee to take. Most encroachment at penalty-kicks occurs near or around the penalty-area arc. One could conclude, therefore, that the referee's difficulty in establishing and/or maintaining match control is likely to

Diagram 6a

DIAGONAL SYSTEM SYSTEM OF CONTROL
FREE-KICK
(midfield)

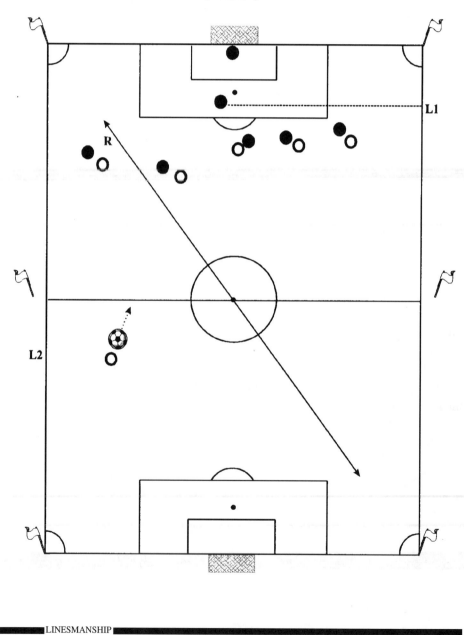

Diagram 6b

DIAGONAL SYSTEM OF CONTROL
FREE-KICK
(outside the penalty-area, near goal)

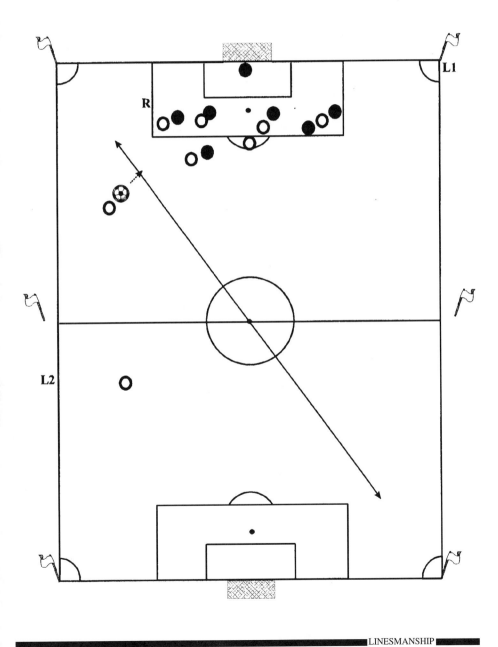

Diagram 7

DIAGONAL SYSTEM OF CONTROL
PENALTY-KICK

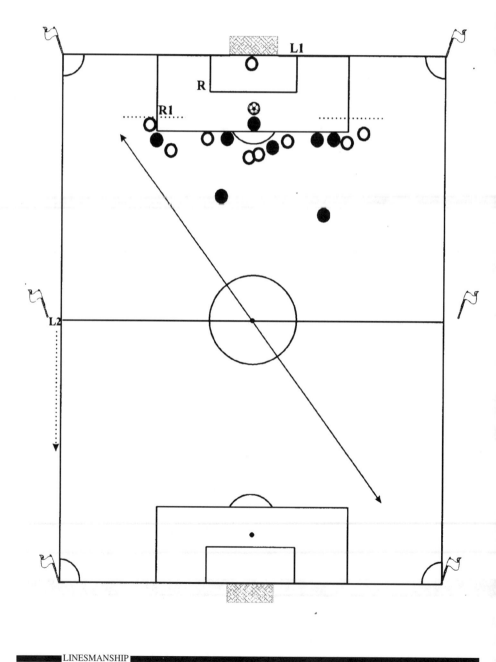

increase when he stands on the goal-line at the taking of a penalty-kick.

This leaves Linesman L2 to stand at the halfway-line where he is in position to assist the referee in the event of a save by the goalkeeper or a rebound from the goal-post or cross-bar, followed by a clearance or counter-attack.

Throw-in

Finally, we come to throw-ins. There are at least two things that have to be considered in determining where the referee and linesmen should position themselves at throw-ins, namely, over which touch-line and in which half of the field did the ball go out of play, and which official will be responsible for watching hand and foot faults by the thrower.

In the Diagonal System of Control, referees almost invariably assume responsibility for hand faults by ensuring that the thrower, while facing the field of play, uses both hands in delivering the ball from behind and over his head in one continuous motion. The linesman patrolling the touch-line from which the throw-in is to be taken is usually responsible for foot faults (the thrower must have part of each foot either on the touch-line or on the ground outside the touch-line), as well as for eventual off-side. (Remember that, according to Paragraph 3(b) of Law XI, a player shall not be declared off-side if he receives the ball direct from a throw-in).

Assume, as in Diagram 8a, that the throw-in is to be taken from the touch-line which is patrolled by Linesman L1 and in that half of the field which he is supervising. Without interfering with the thrower, Linesman L1 stands in his basic position, that is, in line with the second last defender, indicating which team is entitled to the throw-in and the place from which the ball shall be thrown in.

The referee (R) moves off his diagonal and towards Linesman L1 so that he is closer to the attackers and the defenders who will be challenging for the ball after the throw-in. The referee is also in a relatively better position to watch for hand faults by the thrower. Linesman L2 stands in his basic position, prepared to assist the referee in the event of a counter-attack, and watching for off-the-ball incidents that may escape the referee.

When the ball goes out of play for a throw-in from the touch-line that is patrolled by Linesman L1, but in the half of the field that is supervised by Linesman L2, the referee assumes the responsibility for indicating which team is entitled to the throw-in. If the referee is in doubt, he will look to Linesman L1 for help, in which case Linesman L1 will act as if the ball went into touch in the half of the field that he is supervising. In any event, the referee positions himself to judge both hand and foot faults, temporarily stepping off the pitch, if necessary, while both linesmen assume their basic positions along the touch-line.

When the throw-in is to be taken from the touch-line that is patrolled by Linesman L2, but in the half of the field that is supervised by Linesman L1, both

Diagram 8a

DIAGONAL SYSTEM OF CONTROL
THROW-IN

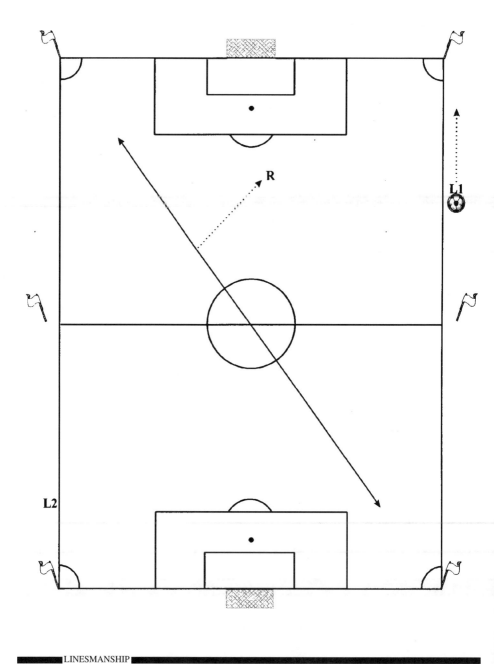

Diagram 8b

DIAGONAL SYSTEM OF CONTROL
THROW-IN

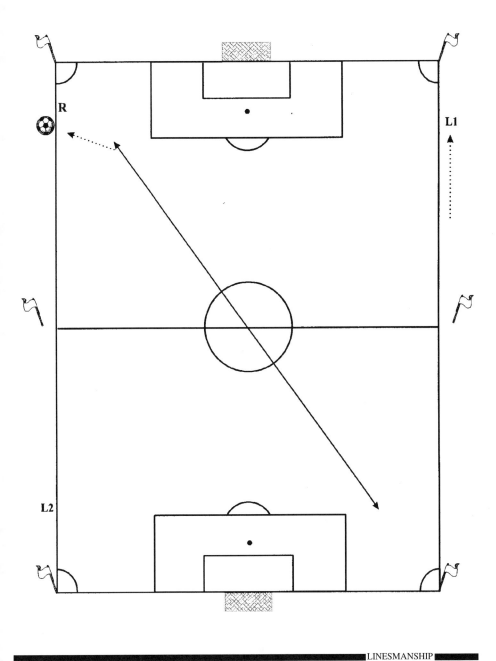

Linesman L2, but in the half of the field that is supervised by Linesman L1, both linesmen assume their basic positions. See Diagram 8b. The referee moves off his diagonal and towards the touch-line to judge both hand and foot faults. He should position himself with Linesman L2 in full view so that the latter may be able to provide assistance, if necessary. Not only is Linesman L1 in position to judge eventual off-side, but he is able to see off-the-ball incidents that may occur before the referee turns to follow play.

COMMUNICATION

Introductory Remarks

The movement and positioning of a referee and his linesmen as one of two main factors upon which the success of the Diagonal System of Match Control depends was discussed in the previous section. The other factor - communication between the three match officials - is discussed in this section.

There are a number of fundamental signals that makeup the language of communication between match officials. The movement and positioning of these officials are often signals in themselves, and, of course, there is the whistle - the most important signal of all, even though it is never mentioned in the Laws of the Game. Indeed, there is only one signal that is specifically mentioned in the Laws, and it is described in International Board Decision 1 of Law XIII (Free-kick) where it is stated that in order to distinguish between a direct and an indirect free-kick, the referee, when he awards an indirect free-kick, shall indicate accordingly by raising an arm above his head. Our emphasis in this section is, however, the flag signals of the linesmen, although reference is made to the hand signals of the referee, as well as to the "silent" signals that referees and linesmen have discovered are essential to match control.

Before proceeding further, it is very important to note that, unless otherwise stated, the signals described in the next two sections are the only official ones approved by the International Football Association Board. So why are "silent" signals dealt with, or even necessary?

In its memorandum on "Signals By The Referee And Linesmen" in the 1995 edition of **LAWS OF THE GAME**, FIFA notes that steps by the referee to improve communication between himself and the players ". . .should be encouraged, but the exaggerated miming of offences can be undignified and confusing and should not be used." By extension, since all signals by the linesmen are solely for the information of the referee, common sense suggests that there is absolutely nothing wrong with covert signals between match officials if these signals can assist the referee in his equitable prosecution of a match and thus enhance his match control. After all, isn't much of refereeing common sense?

It is also very important to note that a flag signal by the linesman is nothing more than an opinion expressed by him (except, of course, in those instances where the linesman signals that he wants to talk to the referee). For example, when the linesman raises his flag to indicate an off-side infraction, all he is simply saying to the referee is that "*in my opinion*, you should stop play because there is an attacker standing in an off-side position, involved with active play." In the circumstances, the decision to stop play or to overrule the linesman rests entirely on the referee, and the latter must accept full responsibility for whatever results from that decision.

The referee should never ignore his linesman's signal. Where he decides to overrule the linesman, the referee should acknowledge that he has seen the signal, but that he has decided to allow play to continue. The acknowledgement should be in the form of a pre-determined signal, usually a "thank you" wave that had been discussed by the referee during his pre-game instructions to the linesmen. The acknowledgement could also be a simple nod or even a shake of the head. Whatever, the referee should acknowledge all signals of his linesmen, simply by acceptance or by other overt means.

On the other hand, if overruled, the linesman should not get upset, especially if the referee has been honest in his judgement. Instead, the linesman should lower his flag and get on with the game, rather than insist on the referee stopping play. Indeed, flag signals by the linesman should not be sustained for more than three or four seconds, except in the following cases where the signal should be maintained until it is acknowledged by the referee:

- ball out of play over the touch-line or goal-line
- misconduct of a serious nature not observed by the referee (especially "off-the-ball" incidents)
- off-side infraction still in effect

Where one linesman has an upraised flag for some time and the referee has not seen it, the other linesman should also flag to attract the referee's attention, and, at the stoppage, point towards the colleague who signalled first.

Let us make a few more points before we move on to an examination of the signals used by the referee and linesmen.

(a) When not signalling, a linesman should always carry his flag unfurled, at his side, and pointed towards the ground. The flag should be visible to the referee at all times, and not hidden behind the linesman's back.
(b) To avoid the embarrassment of his flag literally "flying off the handle", a linesman should ensure that it is securely attached to the flagstick. By the same token, a linesman who is short in stature should be careful not to inadvertently step on his flag when running with it.

(c) A linesman should avoid flag movements that may be mistaken by the referee for signals. Accordingly, linesmen are advised to avoid carrying the flag above waist-level as they patrol the touch-lines and goal-lines. Furthermore, superfluous waving and showiness are to be avoided.

(d) Linesmen should stop and face the field of play when signalling. They should hold the flag in the appropriate hand and away from the body when giving directional signals. This could often mean changing the flag from one hand to another to avoid cross-body signalling, a manoeuvre that should not be difficult for linesmen with flag-handling dexterity.

(e) Apart from those instances where it is necessary for him to give a quick signal to indicate that the ball has gone out of play, a linesman should always look to the referee before giving him a flag signal. He should refrain being "flag-happy". Instead, before signalling, the linesman should ask himself such questions as:

• Does the referee want my signal?
• If I do not signal, will I embarrass the referee?
• If I do not signal, will the game fall into disrepute?
• Will my lack of a signal result in match control problems for the referee?

If the answer to any of the questions asked above is Yes, then the linesman should provide a signal to the referee.

Signals By The Referee

The signals that have been approved by the International Football Association Board for referees are illustrated in Figure 1. It is important to note that these signals are not only for the benefit of players, team officials and spectators; they are also for the benefit of the linesmen who, in turn, may have to go through a series of movements and positionings in preparation of the next sequence of plays.

For example, following a whistle by the referee and his signal for a corner-kick, Linesman L1 in the attacking zone will position himself as illustrated in Diagram 4. Similarly, when the referee signals that he has awarded an indirect free-kick to the attacking team, the linesmen will be aware that a goal cannot be scored direct from the resulting kick, and that if the ball enters the defending team's goal before it is played or touched by a second player, the next action in the game will be a goal-kick. In the circumstances, the linesmen will position themselves for the goal-kick as shown in Diagram 3.

Obviously, the simpler and clearer the signals of the referee, the easier it will be for the linesmen to understand what the referee is doing and, just as important, what exactly he wants them to do to assist him. This is the essence of effective

Figure 1

APPROVED SIGNALS BY THE REFEREE

GOAL-KICK

CORNER-KICK

CAUTION (yellow card)
DISMISSAL (red card)

PENALTY-KICK

INDIRECT FREE-KICK

DIRECT FREE-KICK

PLAY ON! ADVANTAGE

communication between a referee and his linesmen.

There is, however, another side to communication between match officials. Just as important as the referee's signals are those by the linesmen to indicate off-side, goal-kick, corner-kick, throw-in, substitution, the occurrence of an infraction which the referee has not seen, a desire to discuss an important issue with the referee, or that a goal has been scored.

Signals By The Linesmen

When an offence which may have escaped the notice of the referee occurs and there is need to bring it to his attention, or when the linesman wants the referee to stop play to deal with an important matter (for example, misconduct by team officials on the bench), the linesman will raise his flag vertically and to its fullest extent as in Figure 2 to attract the referee's attention. This is the basic signal of the linesman.

Off-side

As soon as the linesman determines that the player who is in an off-side position is involved in active play (that is, he is interfering with play or with an opponent, or that he is gaining an advantage by being in that position), he will raise his flag vertically to indicate to the referee that an off-side infringement has occurred. Once the referee stops play for the infringement, the linesman will lower his flag at full arm's length and point it across the field of play as in Figure 3(a), 3(b), or 3(c) to indicate to the referee the location from which the indirect free-kick is to be taken. The linesman will maintain that signal until the ball is correctly placed.

As mentioned earlier, should the referee fail to see the linesman's signal for off-side, the linesman will lower his flag after three or four seconds and get on with the game. If, however, a goal results directly after the off-side infringement, the linesman will stand at attention, rather than give the referee the standard signal to indicate the scoring of a valid goal, that is, running towards the halfway-line. Clearly, if the ball is played several times after the missed off-side infringement, the linesman will not bring the infringement to the referee's attention if a goal is scored.

Goal, Goal-kick and Corner-kick

When the ball goes out of play over the goal-line, play may be restarted either with a kick-off, a goal-kick or a corner-kick.

Let us deal with the situation where the whole of the ball passes over the goal-line, between the goal-posts and under the cross-bar, that is, the essence of Law X. If the linesman believes that a goal has been scored and the referee has not already stopped play, he should raise his flag vertically and decisively to indicate

APPROVED SIGNALS BY THE LINESMAN

Figure 2

ATTENTION!
INFRINGEMENT!

APPROVED SIGNALS BY THE LINESMAN

Figure 3(a)
OFF-SIDE
On the far side of the field

Figure 3(b)
OFF-SIDE
Near the centre of the field

Figure 3(c)
OFF-SIDE
On the near side of the field

to the referee that the ball has gone out of play. Almost instantaneously, and while looking at the referee, the linesman will sprint along the touch-line towards the halfway-line. This movement by the linesman will be confirmation to the referee that a goal has been scored.

If the linesman believes that the goal should not be awarded (that is, in situations covered in Law X by the phrase "Except as otherwise provided by these Laws. . ."), he will stand still with his flag pointing downwards to indicate to the referee that something occurred which should cancel the goal.The linesman will remain in that position, motionless, until the referee checks with him (sometimes by coming over to talk to him, but preferably communicating by means of a pre-arranged "silent" signal), or waves him back upfield, or the ball is kicked-off. Once the game is restarted, the goal cannot be cancelled (IBD 6 of Law V), so the linesman should resume his basic position on the touch-line.

> **The foregoing points to a very good reason why a referee and his linesmen should maintain eye contact with each other at all times. The corollary to this statement is that a referee should never award a goal before looking at the linesman for assurance that nothing has occurred to invalidate it.**

When the whole of the ball goes over the defending team's goal-line (not between the goal posts) for a goal-kick, that is, it was last played by an attacker, the linesman may again have to signal that the ball went out of play if there is any doubt. If the ball goes out of play over that part of the goal-line nearest to him, the linesman will lower his flag and then point it horizontally towards the goal-area to signal that play should be restarted with a goal-kick. (See Figure 4).

APPROVED SIGNALS BY THE LINESMAN

Figure 4
GOAL-KICK

In signalling for the goal-kick, the linesman should also look at the referee in case the latter has already made a decision which may be different from the linesman's. For example, the referee might have seen the ball deflect from a defender before passing over the goal-line, and he might have already decided to award a corner-kick to the attackers.

If the ball goes out of play over that part of the goal-line that is away from the linesman, he will raise his flag, if necessary, to indicate that the ball is out of play, and he should be ready to signal for a goal-kick or corner-kick if called upon to do so by the referee. If the linesman did not see whether the ball was last played by an attacker or a defender, he will simply lower his flag and stand at attention, perhaps even shake his head slightly or employ some other form of pre-arranged body language to confirm to the referee that he does not know how play should be restarted. In the circumstances, the referee will make his decision unassisted.

When the whole of the ball goes over the goal-line for a corner-kick, the linesman will move towards the corner-flagpost, point to the corner-quadrant with his flag (see Figure 5), and then position himself where the referee instructed him to be at corner-kicks.

Whatever position the linesman assumes at corner-kicks, he will ensure that the ball is correctly placed when the kick is to be taken from the corner-quadrant nearest to him. Generally speaking, the linesman will have no problem having the kicker comply with the requirements of Law XVII. This will be true especially where the linesman possesses great man-management skills. However, where the kicker refuses to place the ball inside the corner-quadrant, the linesman will raise his flag to signal to the referee that all is not well.

If the corner-kick is to be taken from the opposite side of the field, away from the linesman, the referee will supervise the placement of the ball within that corner-quadrant.

Throw-in

When the whole of the ball passes over the touch-line, the linesman will indicate with the basic signal that the ball is out of play. Once again, referees and linesmen are reminded that such a signal would be superfluous if it were obvious that the ball had gone into touch. If the ball goes out of play over that part of the touch-line which the linesman is patrolling and in that half of the field which he is supervising, he will give a directional signal to the referee, indicating which team shall take the throw-in. This directional signal will consist of the flag being held at a 45-degree angle above the horizontal towards the goal which is to be or should be attacked, as illustrated in Figure 6.

If the ball goes over the touch-line which the linesman is patrolling, but in that part of the field for which the referee is responsible, the referee will indicate which team will take the throw-in, unless he looks to the linesman for help. In the

APPROVED SIGNALS BY THE LINESMAN

Figure 5

CORNER-KICK

Figure 6

THROW-IN

circumstances, and assuming that he is certain which team should take the throw-in, the linesman will act as if the ball had gone into touch in his half of the field, and he will give a directional signal to the referee. Where a linesman has no idea which team should take the throw-in, he will only indicate to the referee that the ball has gone out of play beyond the touch-line, and he will allow the referee to decide whose throw-in it is.

From the foregoing, one would certainly conclude that there was a complete breakdown in communication if the referee, near the play, signalled for a throw-in in one direction, while the linesman, well downfield, signalled in the opposite direction! In terms of match control, many a game has come apart at the seams as a result of poor communication between the referee and his linesmen. That said, it is well to point out that, in almost all circumstances, the referee should accept the linesman's flag for out-balls and throw-ins, unless the direction given by the linesman for a throw-in is so obviously incorrect. This acceptance is part of the mutual referee/linesman support mechanism. It is also a great confidence-builder for linesmen.

APPROVED SIGNALS BY THE LINESMAN

Figure 7

SUBSTITUTION

Substitution

Until July 5, 1982, there was no distinct signal by linesmen to indicate to the referee that a substitution was to be made. They simply raised their flag vertically to signal to the referee that a substitution was desired. This was, of course, the same signal that they employed whenever they had to indicate to the referee that the game should be stopped.

At its Annual General Meeting in Madrid on July 6, 1982, the International Football Association Board approved a distinct signal for linesmen's use at substitutions. A new paragraph was added to the section on "Co-operation between Linesmen and Referee", and it was published in the 1983 edition of the **LAWS OF THE GAME AND UNIVERSAL GUIDE FOR REFEREES** in the following manner:

"5. Substitution. When a substitution is to be made, the linesman nearest to the point of substitution shall attract the attention of the referee by raising his flag as shown in the illustration included in 'Signals by the Linesmen. . ."

The front view of the signal for substitution that was approved by the Board, and is in present use, is illustrated in Figure 7.

The linesman will maintain the signal for substitution until the attention of the referee is obtained and the substitution is completed, that is, according to Paragraph 5(f) of Law III, " . . .when the substitute enters the field of play, from which moment he becomes a player and the player whom he is replacing ceases to be a player." When the referee has his back to the linesman nearest the point of substitution, and is, therefore, unaware that a substitution is desired, the other linesman will attract the referee's attention by raising his flag as illustrated in Figure 7.

"Silent" Signals

So far, we have discussed the overt signals of the referee and the linesmen. We have also emphasized that these signals are the only ones that have been approved by the International Football Association Board for use by registered referees of national associations that are affiliated to FIFA.

There are, however, several signals that are used by the referee and his linesmen to communicate with each other without the players and spectators being aware that the match officials are conducting a silent conversation. These signals are commonly referred to as "silent" signals.

Perhaps the great advantage in using "silent" signals is that players and spectators alike are seldom aware of any disagreement when a referee overrules a linesman. This is especially so where the linesman accepts the referee's decision without gesture or comment, and simply gets on with the game. Still, it needs pointing out that in order to avoid confusion during a match, "silent" signals, like all other signals, should be simple and clear. Obviously, a nod or a shake of the head is as simple and as clear as these signals need to be.

At the risk of sounding heretical, it also needs pointing out that, irrespective of edicts from FIFA or the International Football Association Board, "silent" signals or any other signals requested in pre-game instructions by the referee should always be respected by the linesman. If something goes wrong, the referee will always be held accountable - unless it was the linesman who failed!

The most commonly used "silent" signals of referees and linesmen are described below.

Goal Scored

Most of what was written earlier regarding movement by a linesman to inform the referee that a goal has been scored is clearly a description of a very effective "silent" signal that is now used throughout the soccer world. For ease of reference, that signal consists of the linesman merely running towards the halfway-line, holding the flagstick at a 45-degree angle below the horizontal, and in advance.

Time Remaining

Referees often ask their linesmen for a signal at any time during the last five minutes of play in each half, or for an indication when time has expired. The number of minutes remaining can be signalled by the linesman extending the appropriate number of fingers against a contrasting background, such as his flag or the white collar or cuffs of his uniform.

When time has expired, the linesman is sometimes asked to place his free arm across his chest, perhaps with the hand covering his badge, or to make some similar pre-arranged signal which the referee should acknowledge. But this begs the following question: Why, if he had already given a signal to the referee during the last five minutes of play, should it still be necessary for a linesman to signal that time has expired?

It must be remembered, though, that these time signals by the linesman are for the guidance of the referee only. According to Paragraph (c) of Law V, the referee is the official timekeeper who shall ". . . allow the full or agreed time, adding thereto all time lost through accident or other cause."

Some referees ask linesmen to place their flag across their chest to indicate that time has expired (see Figure 8). This signal should obviously be stricken from the linesman's repertoire, for it is precisely the same one that many referees instruct their linesmen to use to indicate that a defender has committed a penal offence within his penalty-area. In the heat of the moment, there is simply no place for a signal with a dual purpose!

OTHER SIGNALS BY THE LINESMAN

Figure 8

TIME-UP!
PENALTY!

Figure 9

OUTSIDE THE
PENALTY AREA

Figure 10

INSIDE THE
PENALTY AREA

Offence

As implied earlier, the linesman shall not signal for an infringement that was clearly within the immediate view of the referee. Where the referee suspects that something is amiss, but he has no clear view of the incident, he may look enquiringly to the linesman who will raise his flag to indicate that the game should be stopped.

If the game is to be restarted by means of a free-kick, the linesman will indicate with a directional signal (as in Figure 6) which team shall take the kick. Furthermore, he will indicate to the referee by means of some pre-arranged signal whether the infringement is to be punished by a direct or an indirect free-kick.

Clearly, the foregoing are overt signals. Where the infringement is to be punished by a penalty-kick, the linesman can communicate this information to the referee with an effective "silent" signal. For example, as soon as the referee stops play, the linesman will lower his flag and, while looking at the referee, immediately move briskly as if to indicate that he is about to assume the position of Linesman L1 in Diagram 7.

Ball In/Out Of The Penalty-area

There is an occasion in the career of every referee when he stops play for an offence, but is uncertain whether the offence occurred inside or outside the penalty-area. There is hardly a problem if the resulting free-kick is to be awarded to the defending team. The difficulty arises when the kick is to be taken by the attackers, and especially if the offence was a foul, punishable by means of a direct free-kick or a penalty-kick. At a time like this, a linesman who is ready and willing to assist is worth his weight in gold!

If the offence occurred outside the penalty-area, the linesman will stand directly in line with the location of the offence. Furthermore, he will hold his flag as surreptitiously as possible across his thighs, with the top of the flag pointing downfield, and away from the penalty-area. See Figure 9. This manoeuvre may mean changing the flag from one hand to another so that the flag is kept in its entirety against the thighs, and not jutting out from the linesman's side.

If the offence took place within the penalty-area, the linesman will use either of two "silent" signals, as instructed by the referee before the match. While looking at the referee, the linesman will move briskly towards the corner-flagpost as if to indicate that he is about to assume a position on the goal-line where it meets the penalty-area. This is the "silent" signal that the FIFA Referees' Committee appears to favor in the circumstances. Alternatively, the linesman will stand at attention, in line with the location of the offence, with his flag held across his thighs and pointing to the corner-flagpost. See Figure 10.

Linesman Waved To The Goal-line

At free-kicks to be taken by the attackers inside or just outside the defending team's penalty-area, referees prefer to stand in line with the "wall", which often is the on-side/off side line, and to wave the linesman down to the goal-line to act as a goal judge. Most referees employ ". . .a flat, palm-downward karate-type gesture parallel to the ground" in sending the linesman to the goal-line. This gesture is seldom seen by players and spectators. Indeed, many a linesman has been known to miss it, even though referees and linesmen are constantly reminded by instructors and assessors that eye contact at all times is a key to effective communication between match officials.

"Free Hand" Signals

Occasionally, one notices linesmen using the "free hand", that is, the one without the flag, to indicate to the referee that "Nothing has happened! ", that the ball has not passed over the goal-line or the touch-line, or that the Advantage Clause should be invoked. Fortunately, the use of "free hand" signals by linesmen is becoming increasingly rare. Perhaps more to the point, fewer referees are instructing their linesmen to use "free hand" signals.

The flag is the main communications tool of the linesman. Every movement of the flag above the linesman's waist tells or should tell a story. If the flag is held unfurled at the linesman's side, pointing downwards and clearly in view of the referee, isn't that a sufficient indication to the referee that all's well? Why, in the circumstances, should there be need of another signal? Why introduce another signal that may confuse the referee in the heat of the game? Furthermore, why should a linesman, with absolutely no authority to do so, take upon himself to overtly apply the Advantage Clause, when it is specifically stated in Paragraph (b) of Law V that it is only the referee who has the discretionary power to do so?

Imagine the confusion that would reign and the embarrassment that would result if, on a foul tackle, a linesman were to demonstratively "apply" the Advantage, while the referee was stopping play to deal with the offence which he felt could jeopardize his match control!

The moral of the story is that a linesman should avoid using his "free hand" to signal to the referee when a flag signal or "silent" signal, for that matter, would achieve the same end.

Summary And Conclusions

With neutral linesmen in support", referees should adopt the Diagonal System of Match Control, which is the most efficient technique yet devised for optimum field coverage by the three match officials. Undoubtedly, the greatest asset of the system is that no part of the field of play is left unpatrolled at any time. Accordingly, on fast counter-attacks, there is always one official up with play.

The linesman should give clear, crisp and accurate signals to the referee, and he should face the field of play when signaling . . .

. . .he should hold the flag in the appropriate hand to avoid cross-body signaling, follow the ball to the goal-line on all occasions, and avoid running on the touch-line, thus reducing the chance of damaging the line . . .

. . .when not signalling, the linesman should carry the flag unfurled, at his side, in clear view of the referee, and pointed towards the ground. . .

. . .he should assist the referee in administering the Laws of the Game at all times and, above all, he should maintain constant eye contact with the referee.

The success of the system is largely dependent upon two main factors, namely, the movement and positioning of the referee and his two linesmen, and the communication between the three. Signals, whether they be overt or covert, make up the language of this communication, although it should be emphasized that the movement and positioning of the referee and the linesmen are often signals in themselves.

It should also be emphasized that a flag signal by the linesman is almost always nothing more than an opinion expressed by him. Accordingly, the decision to stop play rests entirely on the referee, and he alone must accept full responsibility for whatever results from that decision.

The Diagonal System of Match Control is likely to breakdown if, for example:

- the referee and a linesman are in the same place at the same time, performing the same task
- the linesmen fail to bring to the attention of the referee misconduct that may not have been observed by him
- the referee ignores the signals of his linesmen
- the referee positions himself with no view of the linesman in the attacking zone
- there is inadequate or no pre-game instruction by the referee to his linesmen, and the linesmen fail to ask for any
- there is no communication whatsoever between the referee and either both linesmen, or even one of them

All the same, when being operated efficiently, the Diagonal System of Match Control confirms, more than anything else, the notion that the referee and his two linesmen constitute the Third Team in a soccer match.

Chapter 4

Off-Side

Introduction

Soccer, we are often told, is a sport that seemingly drives everyone associated with it into a frenzy. This is obviously an exaggeration. What is not an exaggeration is that Law XI, which deals with off-side, is by far the most controversial of the seventeen laws that make up the Laws of the Game. It is also the law that has arguably been the most difficult to finalize and that has undergone the most change since it first appeared, *circa* 1856, in the Cambridge University Rules as follows:

> *"RULE 9: If the ball has passed a player, and has come from the direction of his own goal, he may not touch it till the other side have kicked it. . . No player is allowed to loiter between the ball and the adversaries' goal."*

There are two important points in the above. The first, which is stated explicitly, is that a player was not allowed to loiter (that is, linger, wait, idle, loaf, lag, dawdle, hang about, or travel indolently) between the ball and the opponents' goal-line. The second point is the implicit statement that, fundamentally, a player was not allowed to interfere with play if he found himself nearer his opponents' goal-line than the ball.

These same points were also included by Reverend J.C. Thring in his 1862 rules of "The Simplest Game" in the following manner:

> *"Rule 9. A player is 'out of play' immediately he is in front of the ball and must return behind the ball as soon as possible. If the ball is kicked by his own side past a player who is 'out of play', he may not touch it or advance. . .",*

and in Law 6 of The Football Association Laws of 1873 as follows:

> *"When a player kicks the ball, any one of the same side who, at such a moment of kicking, is nearer to the opponents' goal-line is out of play, and may not touch the ball himself, nor in any way whatever prevent any other player from doing so. . ."*

Basis Of The Law

Out of the foregoing emerged what was the basis of the Off-side Law, namely, that a player was in an off-side position (or "out of play", as Thring and The Football Association described it) if he were nearer to the opponents' goal-line than the ball.

Establishing The Facts

When, in 1938, Sir Stanley Rous re-modeled the Laws of the Game in their present form, Law XI was devoted to off-side. Up to that time and since then, the Off-side Law underwent and has undergone several rewordings. Yet, in spite of the changes that have been effected in the law by the International Football Association Board, there are still two stages, one of **fact**, the other of **opinion**, upon which to decide whether a player is or is not off-side.

In other words, the basis of the Off-side Law has not changed one iota since it was first published in the Cambridge University Rules almost 140 years ago. As is evident from Law XI in the 1995 edition of FIFA's **LAWS OF THE GAME**, a player is still in an off-side position if he is nearer his opponents' goal-line than the ball *at the moment the ball is touched or played by a member of his own team*. And that is a fact! Expressed another way, a player cannot be in an off-side position if he is behind the ball when it is last played by a teammate. Indeed, a player who is even with the ball cannot be in an off-side position. That, also, is a fact!

It is likewise a fact that, in certain circumstances, a player may obtain relief from his off-side position. Thus, according to Paragraph 1 of Law XI, a player will be relieved from his off-side position if:

(a) he is in his own half of the field of play, or
(b) if he is not nearer to his opponents' goal-line than at least two of his opponents.

As a statement, Relief (a) is relatively straightforward. It needs little elaboration, except to emphasize that, according to IBD 1 of Law IX, the lines marking the field of play are part of the areas of which they are boundaries. The halfway-line is, therefore, a part of each half of the field of play. That being the case, whereas a player who is standing with both feet on the halfway-line, but not extending into his opponents' half of the field, is considered for purposes of Law XI to be in his own half of the field of play, he could be in an off-side position if he were standing with one foot in each half of the field of play. See Diagram 9. All the same, referees should not become preoccupied with this technical point, but should instead place more emphasis in their field performance on a sensible administration of IBD 8 of Law V.

LAW XI
Off-Side

1. A player is in an off-side position if he is nearer to his opponents' goal-line than the ball, unless:
    (a) he is in his own half of the field of play, or
    (b) he is not nearer to his opponents' goal-line than at least two of his opponents.

2. It is not an offence in itself to be in an off-side position. A player shall only be penalized for being in an off-side position if, at the moment the ball touches, or is played by one of his team, he is, in the opinion of the referee, involved in active play by:
    (a) interfering with play, or
    (b) interfering with an opponent, or
    (c) gaining an advantage by being in that position.

3. A player shall not be declared off-side by the referee
    (a) merely because of his being in an off-side position, or
    (b) if he receives the ball direct from a goal-kick, a corner-kick, or a throw-in.

4. If a player is declared off-side, the referee shall award an indirect free-kick, which shall be taken by a player of the opposing team from where the infringement occurred, unless the offence is committed by a player in his opponents' goal-area, in which case the free-kick shall be taken from any point within the goal-area.

DECISIONS OF THE INTERNATIONAL F.A. BOARD

(1) Off-side shall not be judged at the moment the player in question receives the ball, but at the moment when the ball is passed to him by one of his own side. A player who is not in an off-side position when one of his colleagues passes the ball to him or takes a free-kick, does not therefore become off-side if he goes forward during the flight of the ball.

(2) A player who is level with the second last opponent or with the last two opponents is not in an off-side position.

Diagram 9

**Whereas Player A can be in an off-side position,
Player B cannot possibly be.**

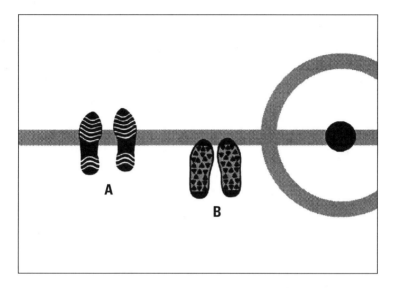

Incidentally, it is interesting to note that, because the off-side position became restricted to the opponents' half of the field of play in 1907, the International Football Association Board decided in 1908 that a flag on a post not less than 5 feet high may be placed opposite the halfway-line on each side of the field of play, not less than 1 yard outside the touch-line. This decision is now part of the text of Law I.

Although Relief (b) is, as a statement, also relatively straightforward, it is clarified in IBD 2 of Law XI which states that a player who is level with the second last opponent or with the last two opponents is not in an off-side position. This is, of course, the same as saying that a player is not in an off-side position if there are at least two opponents **as near their goal line** as he is. And that is a fact!

Consider Diagrams 10 and 11 in which A and B are attackers, Y and Z are defenders, and X is the defending goalkeeper. In Diagram 10, A is in possession of the ball. Seeing Y in front of him, A passes the ball to B, who, *at the moment the ball is last touched or played by A*, is not in an off-side position because he is not nearer to his opponents' goal-line than at least two opponents (X and Z). In Diagram 11, A passes the ball to B. Again, B is not in an off-side position, because he is level with defender Z and the defending goalkeeper, X, *at the moment the ball is last touched or played by A.*

Diagram 10

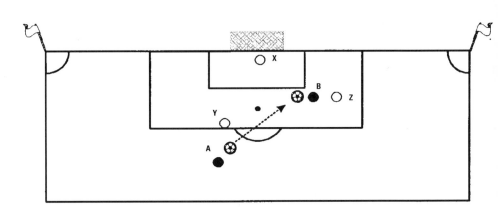

Diagram 11

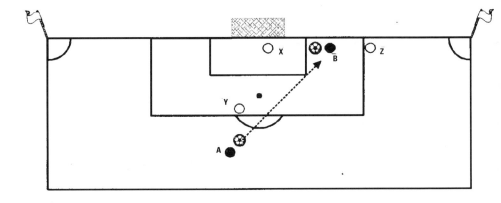

In the diagrams above, Attacker B is not in an off-side position at *the moment the ball is last played by teammate A.*

Finally, note from Paragraph 3(b) of Law XI that there is no breach of the law if a player who is in an off-side position receives the ball direct from a goal-kick, a corner-kick or a throw-in. That, too, is a fact!

The foregoing is summarized on the left-hand side of the accompanying Off-side Chart which has been adapted from a flow chart in the book, **FAIR OR FOUL?**, by Paul E. Harris Jr. and Larry R. Harris.

The Off-Side Chart

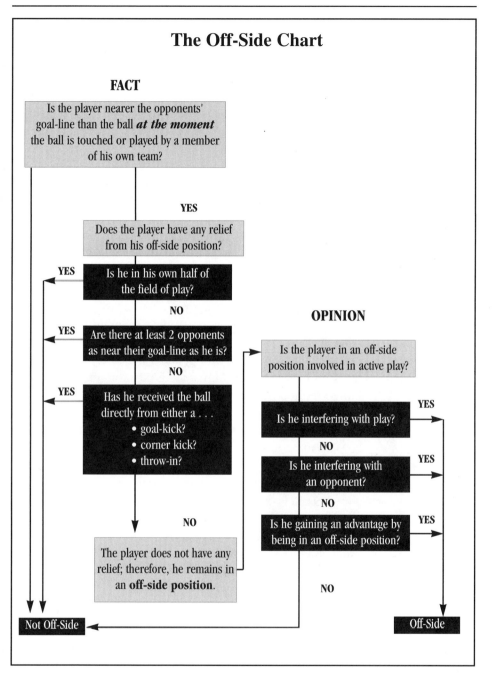

FACT

Is the player nearer the opponents' goal-line than the ball *at the moment* the ball is touched or played by a member of his own team?

YES

Does the player have any relief from his off-side position?

YES Is he in his own half of the field of play?

NO

OPINION

YES Are there at least 2 opponents as near their goal-line as he is?

NO

Is the player in an off-side position involved in active play?

YES Has he received the ball directly from either a . . .
- goal-kick?
- corner kick?
- throw-in?

Is he interfering with play? **YES**

NO

Is he interfering with an opponent? **YES**

NO

NO

Is he gaining an advantage by being in an off-side position? **YES**

The player does not have any relief; therefore, he remains in an **off-side position**.

NO

Not Off-Side

Off-Side

Formulating The Opinion

Once he deems that a player who is in an off-side position has no relief from that position, the referee moves to the next stage in his decision-making process, namely, forming an opinion as to whether the player is taking advantage of his off-side position. Indeed, neutral linesmen, who have the delegated responsibility of indicating to the referee whether a player is offending Law XI, also have to form an opinion as to whether the player in an off-side position is taking advantage of that position.

Why must this opinion be formed? It is because it is not an offence for a player to be in an off-side position, neither is it an offence for him to go into nor remain in that position. According to Paragraph 2 of Law XI, it only becomes an offence if, *at the moment the ball is touched or played by one of his team*, a player is, in the opinion of the referee, influencing the game, hampering an opponent, or gaining an advantage while in an off-side position. In other words, he is involved in so-called active play.

What, then, are likely to be the considerations of a referee (and of a neutral linesman, for that matter) when he is forming an opinion as to whether a player is influencing the game, or is hampering an opponent, or is gaining an advantage while he is in an off-side position? If, for example, the player is involved or could readily become involved in the play, or if an opponent is acutely aware of his presence or is distracted by his potentially threatening position, or if the player deliberately moves into a position to receive the ball, or if he calls for the ball or obstructs an opponent, then the player should be declared off-side. In short, as decided by the International Football Association Board in 1924, if the player by his actions causes the play to be affected, he should be penalized. All of this is summarized on the right-hand side of the Off-side Chart.

The considerations described above appear to be quite simple. Yet, they are the very ones for which there is lack of unanimity among referees, players, team officials, spectators - indeed, the lot, - and which make Law XI the controversial one that so many people believe it to be. For example, when referees are faced in classrooms with off-side situations on flip charts, magnetic boards or videos, or when as a group they are watching a match from the stands, it is not uncommon to hear them disagree in deciding whether a player who was in an off-side position was hampering or obstructing an opponent. For their part, most spectators leave the impression that they are unaware of the vast difference between off-side position and off-side.

As to the players, it appears that most of the time when they are declared off-side, they routinely protest to the referee that they were not nearer to the opponents' goal-line than at least two of their opponents. The rest of the time they remind the referee of IBD 1 of Law XI, which states that off-side shall be judged *at the moment the ball is played by a teammate* and not when it is received by the offending player. Little wonder that referees and linesmen are so often criticized for their interpretation of Law XI!

If one follows the FACT-OPINION continuum in the Off-side Chart, it will be easy to appreciate the rationale used by the International Football Association Board when, in 1979, it excised that part of the text which stated that a player in an off-side position could not be declared off-side if the ball had last been played by an opponent. In other words, if the referee deems that a player is in an off-side position *at the moment the ball is last played or touched by a member of his own team* (FACT), and if, in the OPINION of the referee, the player is gaining an advantage or is interfering with play or an opponent ("interference" includes mannerisms, use of voice, as well as movement or motion, but not in the form of physical offence covered under Law XII), the referee shall rule that the player is off-side. The fact that the ball may later strike an opponent will not legitimize the off-side, for off-side occurs *at the moment the ball is last played by a teammate.*

Dr. Eric Sellin expresses this latter point very nicely in his book, **THE INNER GAME OF SOCCER,** when he observes that "It is at the instant that the first player 'plays' the ball that the relative field positions of the ball, the attackers and the defenders become relevant to Law XI..." In this case, Sellin continues, "the punishable event by definition *precedes* the intervention which supposedly made it not punishable!"

In support of his argument, Sellin quotes former FIFA Referee Instructor, Diego De Leo, who writes in his book, **REGOLE DEL CALCIO,** that "The illegal position of an attacking player is remedied by the intervention of a defender touching the ball only if, in the referee's judgement, this attacking player was not taking part in the action. Otherwise the offside should be punished, even if the referee's whistle is not blown in time."

Punishment

The punishment for being adjudged off-side is the award of an indirect free-kick which shall be taken by a player of the opposing team from where the offence occurred, subject to the overriding conditions imposed in Law XIII.

But where does the offence of off-side occur? Is it at the on-side/off-side line? That is to say, is it at the halfway-line (remember that a player cannot be off-side if he is in his own half of the field of play), or the line of at least the two last defenders (remember, too, that a player cannot be off-side if there are at least two opponents as near their goal-line as he is), or in line with the ball (finally, remember that a player cannot be off-side if he is level with the ball or is behind it when it is last played by a teammate)? See Diagram 12.

Diagram 12

ON-SIDE/OFF-SIDE LINES

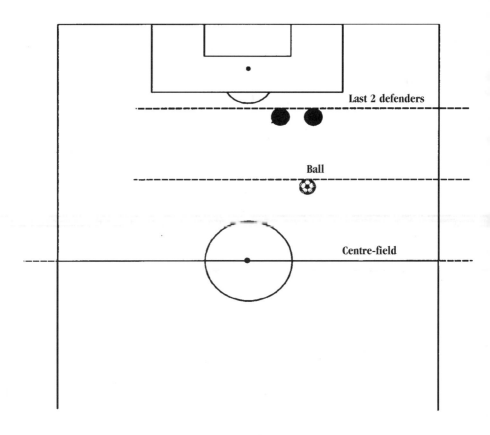

According to Law XI, it is clear that the offence occurs at the spot where the player is standing in an off-side position and at which position the referee considers him to be interfering with play or with an opponent, or to be gaining an advantage by being in that position. In other words, although practice has proven otherwise, the offence does not always occur in line with the place where the linesman is standing with his flag raised above his head to indicate that the player is off-side.

Advice To Linesmen

After all is said and done, the most important task of a neutral linesman is to judge off-side, except where the referee replaces him in this function by sending him to the goal-line to act as a goal judge. Accordingly, a linesman should deal with off-side on the field of play as though he were refereeing the match. That is to say, he should only raise his flag for off side, not simply because a player is in an off-side position!

As FIFA puts it, before raising his flag to indicate to the referee that a player is off-side, the linesman must be certain that the player is:

- involved in active play, or
- interfering with an opponent, or
- gaining an advantage by being in an off-side position

Moreover, according to instructions given by FIFA to the referees and linesmen who officiated in the 1994 World Cup Final Tournament, a linesman should decide in favor of the attacker whenever he is in doubt that an off-side infringement has occurred. In other words, in off-side situations, a linesman's maxim should be "If in doubt, no flag!" What has been written so far in this chapter is, therefore, germane to this most important task of a linesman.

Diagrams illustrating points in connection with off-side have purposely been omitted from this chapter. The referee's bible, FIFA's **LAWS OF THE GAME**, contains twenty-two excellent diagrams on the subject. FIFA also has thirty-five diagrams on off-side in the manual it used to instruct the 1994 World Cup referees and linesmen during their training sessions in Dallas, Texas in March, 1994. Stanley Lover has included ten in his latest book, **SOCCER LAWS EXPLAINED**; Denis Howell has six in his **SOCCER REFEREEING**; and Paul and Larry Harris inserted fourteen in their multi-editioned **FAIR OR FOUL?**. Why, then, re-invent the wheel? Instead, linesmen are urged to study these diagrams very carefully and as often as possible, noting that a few of them are no longer correct as a result of recent alterations to Law XI by the International Football Association Board.

There are, however, several more points that a linesman should be aware of in dealing with Law XI, including the following:

(a) For purposes of Law XI, there is absolutely no difference between a player touching and playing the ball.
(b) A player who is not off-side when a corner-kick, goal-kick or throw-in is taken may, without having moved, be off-side as soon as the ball has been played by a teammate.

(c) A player following or in line with a teammate who is in possession of the ball cannot possibly be off-side.

(d) Once judged off-side, a player may not put himself on-side by, say, running back into his own half of the field of play or running beyond the touch-line or the goal-line.

(e) A player may be off-side if he receives the ball direct from his goalkeeper's clearance (as distinct from a goal-kick), for example, from a punt or a throw while the goalkeeper is standing within his penalty-area.

(f) The ball hitting either or both goal-posts, or the cross-bar, or the goal-keeper, or any combination of these agencies and rebounding into the field of play does not put a player on-side who was off-side when the ball was last played by a teammate.

(g) Although a player may stand in an off-side position at the taking of a direct or an indirect free-kick (but not at a penalty-kick), he may be declared off-side as a result of his action immediately after the free-kick has been taken.

(h) There is no off-side if a player is put in an off-side position by an opponent's wilful exit from the field of play; on the contrary, the opponent should be cautioned for ungentlemanly conduct, for his action is contrary to the spirit of fair play.

(i) An attacker cannot be off-side if, at the moment the ball is last played by a teammate, he is standing in a "wall" on the defenders' goal-line.

Summary And Conclusions

The Off-side Law is the most controversial of the Laws of the Game. Yet, as a theoretical construct, it is among the simplest of these laws, based as it is upon the very simple notion that a player is in an off-side position if he is nearer his opponents' goal-line than the ball.

Notwithstanding new concepts that have been introduced into the soccer lexicon in recent months (for example, "area of active play", "active and passive off-side"), there are still in practice only two stages, one of *fact*, the other of *opinion*, upon which to decide whether a player is or is not off-side, and does or does not offend the Off-side Law.

1. *Fact:* what is the position of the player at the moment the ball is touched or played by a teammate?

2. *Opinion*: is the player who is in an off-side position interfering with play or with an opponent, or is he gaining an advantage by being in that position?

The factors which have to be considered by referees and linesmen in their application of Law XI are, therefore, the relative positions of the player in an off-side position, the ball, the defenders, and the attacker with the ball. In most off-side situations, these positions are fluid. It is, however, precisely because these positions can and often do change in the wink of an eye that referees and inesmen need to concentrate intensely when judging off-side situations. This high degree of concentration is crucial for linesmen especially, since their most important task during a match is to judge off-side.

Finally, referees and linesmen should always remember that off-side is judged not at the moment the player in question receives the ball, but, rather, at the moment the ball is passed to him by a teammate. Furthermore, in off-side situations, linesmen should be guided by the maxim "if in doubt, no flag!"

Chapter 5

Our Friends, The Linesmen

A Referee's Appeal

According to Law VI, linesmen shall be appointed to assist the referee to control the game according to the Laws. I do not know why this is so, but I often get the impression that there are quite a number of referees who do not sufficiently appreciate the tremendous assistance that linesmen, especially neutral linesmen, provide to them. For me, too many referees still regard linesmen as mere jobbers. This is an unfortunate attitude for us to adopt towards our colleagues who are our best, and sometimes our only friends at the park, and whose main goal is to make us look good!

A linesman's task is not an easy one, and there are many experts who argue that the art of lining is a more difficult one than that of refereeing. This may well be true. What is certain is that, during a typical match, linesmen more often than not are involved in every facet of the Laws of the Game. We could begin with Law VI, wherein it is stated that linesmen should indicate to the referee when the ball is out of play (Law IX) and which side is entitled to the resulting goal-kick (Law XVI), corner-kick (Law XVII) or throw-in (Law XV). More than that, referees ask linesmen to assist them, by appropriate positions and signals, with the placement of the ball and the position of players at goal-kicks and corner-kicks, and linesmen are instructed to watch for foot faults by those taking throw-ins.

Prior to the commencement of the match, our linesmen co-operate with us by examining the field of play and the appurtenances of the game. They inspect field markings, determine whether flagposts conform to prescribed requirements, and they ascertain whether the goal nets are securely attached to the goal-posts, cross-bars and ground behind the nets, as well as provide ample room for the goalkeeper (Law I). They also make certain that the holes in the goal nets are not large enough to permit the ball to pass through them, and that fasteners used to hold the nets in place on the goal-posts and cross-bars do not pose a danger to anyone participating in the match.

Sometimes linesmen are asked to make a preliminary inspection of the match ball to determine whether it meets the requirements of Law II, and, apart from indicating to the referee when a substitution is desired (Law VI), they often assist him in controlling substitution at the halfway-line along the touch-line (Law III)

Linesmen also co-operate with the referee by inspecting players' footwear and other equipment (Law IV), and they become adept at giving him surreptitious signals to indicate that time in each half is about to expire or has expired (Law VII). Quite often, linesmen are also asked to check team sheets and player identity cards (Law III).

Once the match has started, we depend heavily upon our linesmen, although not too many of us would admit to this fact. Mind you, this dependence is not to be construed as dereliction of our duties. It is simply that, under certain circumstances, we depend upon the opinions that linesmen are capable of giving us as a result of their superior positioning along the touch-line or goal-line. We are still required to make all decisions on the field of play. Thus, we react when our linesmen indicate that not every player is in his own half of the field at the kick-off (Law VIII) or that a goal has been scored (Law X), just as we react when they signal that a player is off-side (Law XI). As a matter of fact, it is in regard to Law XI that we rely most heavily upon our linesmen, since indicating to us whether a player is off side is the most important of the delegated responsibilities that we give to them. And yet, there is no reference in the Laws of the Game to a linesman's responsibility in determining off-side infringements!

At the taking of free-kicks near the defenders' goal, linesmen are often given a pre-arranged signal by the referee to take up a position on the goal-line near the corner-flagpost from where it is possible for them to act as goal judges (Law X). On penalty-kicks, we always ask our linesmen to take up a position along the goal-line so that they may watch the goalkeeper to see that he is standing on his goal-line (Law XIV), and also act as goal judges. At other times when we award free-kicks, we may request our linesmen to assist us with the placement of the ball and/or the position of the players (XIII). Linesmen also become involved in such referee duties as permitting no one but authorized persons to enter the field of play, and noting goal scorers as well as cautions and dismissals (Law V).

Finally, as mentioned earlier, and subject to the decision of the referee, the linesmen's duty is that of assisting the referee in controlling the game in accordance with the Laws. That assistance includes, among other things, bringing to the attention of the referee any contravention of the Laws and especially rough play and ungentlemanly/violent conduct (Law XII).

We ask and we expect our linesmen to perform all these tasks. Most do so in an efficient manner. All do so to the best of their ability, although a majority have probably received practically no coaching in the art of running the line. Surely, we should let our linesmen know in a sincere way that we appreciate their assistance. It is not enough for us to tell them that a referee and his linesmen constitute the Third Team. We must make them feel a part of that team. After all, linesmen are our best friends on the field, aren't they?

Chapter 6

Assessment Criteria
For Linesmen

Introduction

Surprisingly, there is very little in the literature on the training of match officials in the art of running the line. What's more, even less is written about the criteria that should be observed in assessing the strengths and weaknesses of a linesman in a particular match, and in measuring the assistance given by him to the referee in the match concerned. In fact, the section in both the FIFA and CONCACAF Referee Inspector's Report forms that deals with the performance of linesmen in international matches is so cryptic in its directives, that neither form provides sufficient guidance to the beginning inspector in assessing the performance of a linesman.

As is evident below, the assessment of a linesman is a strictly quantitative affair when it is conducted with the use of the FIFA Referee Inspector's Report form. Clearly, it is impossible in this system for one to determine the areas in which a linesman has displayed strengths and weaknesses. Consequently, while the form is adequate for measuring the efficiency of a linesman, it is not too useful a tool for educating him.

The FIFA Form

Linesman											
	1	1	2	3	4	5	6	7	8	9	10
	2	1	2	3	4	5	6	7	8	9	10

The CONCACAF Form

Linesman							
	1	Unsatisfactory		Weak		Good		Excellent
	2						

The CONCACAF Report form, with its very narrow range of subjective indices, is not any better a tool for educating linesmen nor for comparing their performances. Worse, it is impossible in this system for one to know, for example, whether "weak" ranges from, say, 50 to 55 per cent efficiency, or whether "good" translates into a 70 per cent performance, or what is an "average" or a "very good" performance.

As a result of the shortcomings outlined above, I have designed the linesman assessment form that appears overleaf.

The form is designed to do three things - all at once:

(a) measure the efficiency of a linesman;
(b) present assessors with criteria for undertaking this measurement; and
(c) provide national associations with a tool for comparing the abilities of their respective cadre of linesmen.

In designing the form, I have drawn on the work of three authors, namely, Denis Howell, Eric Sellin and Stanley Lover. Their work is cited in the bibliography. I have also been influenced by the linesman assessment form now in use by the English F.A. My greatest influence, though, in designing the form has been my own experience as a FIFA and CONCACAF Match Commissioner.

Elements Of Referee-Linesman Co-operation

What exactly should an assessor be looking for in evaluating the field performance of a linesman? The question could probably best be tackled by first pointing out that, in the case of a referee assessment, an assessor should be looking for the speed with which the referee is able to establish match control, and his ability to maintain that control throughout the duration of play. In the case of a linesman's performance, an assessor should be looking for the degree to which the linesman co-operates with the referee so that the latter can, in turn, achieve a high degree of match control.

From a linesman's point of view, there are several elements that contribute to referee-linesman co-operation. These elements can be grouped under five broad headings, namely:

• Personality
• Fitness, Mobility and Positioning
• Signals
• Man-management
• Overall Co-operation with the Referee

LINESMAN ASSESSMENT FORM

LINESMAN:_____

1. PERSONALITY:
Appearance; attitude; impartiality;
confidence; concentration level;
composure under pressure.

Unsatisfactory 1-5	Fair 6-8	Good 9-11	Very Good 12-14	Excellent 15

MARK [ ]

2. Fitness, Mobility, Positioning:
Lateral, backward and forward
movements; sprinting ability;
acceleration; quickness in
resumption of appropriate positions;
following ball to goal-line.

Unsatisfactory 1-5	Fair 6-8	Good 9-11	Very Good 12-14	Excellent 15

MARK [ ]

3. Signals:
Approved; clear, crisp, prompt and
decisive; flag-handling dexterity; correct
decisions; unnecessary flag or "free hand"
signals.

Unsatisfactory 1-16	Fair 17-25	Good 26-35	Very Good 36-45	Excellent 46-50

(a)   off-side (25 marks max.)
(b)   throw-in (5 marks max.)
(c)   corner-kick (5 marks max.)
(d)   substitution (5 marks max.)
(e)   ball out of play (5 marks max.)
(f)   fouls and misconduct (5 marks max.)

  • as unseen by referee
  • reaction to referee's signals and gestures

MARK [ ]

4. Man-Management:
Effective, sensible, management;
tolerance; advice to players,
substitutes and bench personnel;
fussy or unobtrusive.

Unsatisfactory 1-3	Fair 4-5	Good 6-7	Very Good 8-9	Excellent 10

MARK [ ]

5. Overall Co-operation with Referee:
Fully supportive; unnecessarily intrusive;
maintenance of eye contact; response to
referee's signals and gestures.

Unsatisfactory 1-3	Fair 4-5	Good 6-7	Very Good 8-9	Excellent 10

MARK [ ]

Unsatisfactory 10-49	Fair 50-69	Good 70-79	Very Good 80-89	Excellent 90-100

TOTAL MARK [ ]

It was pointed out in Chapter 3, the heart of this book, that there are two main factors upon which the success of the Diagonal System of Match Control depends, namely, the movement and positioning of a referee and his linesmen, and the communication between the team of match officials. Accordingly, an aggregate of 65 percentage points has been awarded for the signalling of the linesman (50 points) and for his fitness, mobility and positioning (15 points). The linesman has also been accorded a maximum mark of 15 points for his personality (more precisely, the manner in which he uses his personality to carry out his duties), and 10 points each for his man-management abilities on the field of play and the overall manner in which he co-operates with the referee.

1. Personality (15 points maximum)

As society becomes more and more permissive, and players become increasingly rebellious, there is a greater tendency for referee educators and assessors to focus on a linesman's use of his personality to assist the referee in controlling a match. Obviously, if a linesman is improperly dressed for a match, is partial to a particular team, has great difficulty in concentrating on, say, the positions of attackers and defenders relative to the on side/off-side lines, or is unable to maintain his composure under pressure resulting from misconduct by anyone at a game, it is unlikely that he will be respected by players and team officials.

In the circumstances, it is unlikely that the referee would have confidence in the opinions of the linesman, and therein could be the start of a breakdown in referee-linesman co-operation.

As with the assessment of a referee, assessors should remember in their consideration of a linesman's personality that "if one important action (by the linesman) takes place which affects the result of the game, that fact has great importance on the grade given and the grade can't be good." That is to say, if a linesman, intimidated by a team's bench personnel, were to lack the courage to indicate to the referee in the final minute of a tied-game that an attacker on that team was off-side when the ball was kicked into the opponents' goal, his mark under this element of referee-linesman co-operation should not exceed six points. Moreover, since there is a tendency for the elements of referee-linesman co-operation to sustain each other, this action (or lack of action) by the linesman should certainly be reflected on the linesman assessment form under Signals, as well as Overall Co-operation With The Referee.

2. Fitness, Mobility, Positioning (15 points maximum)

The speed of the modern game calls for referees and linesmen alike to possess a high level of fitness. And whereas referees are required to undergo more strenuous physical fitness tests than linesmen, the fact remains that the latter must also be extremely fit and mobile, if only to follow the ball to the goal-line on all occasions, or to move quickly to act as a goal-judge whenever he receives a signal from the referee to do so, or to quickly resume appropriate positions according to the dictates of play. In short, not only must a linesman be able to maintain maximum physical activity for the whole game, but he must also be able to move nimbly along the touch-lines and goal-lines, and sprint whenever the occasion demands it.

3. Signals (50 points maximum)

Not surprisingly, "signals" is the word that quickly comes to mind whenever one thinks of a linesman - the signals he employs to indicate to the referee that a player is off-side, or that the ball has gone out of play beyond the touch-line or goal-line, or that a substitution is desired, and so on.

For assessors who are evaluating Signals as an element of referee-linesman co-operation, there is, however, much more to consider in the performance of a linesman than the mere mechanical aspect of the raising or the lowering of a flag by him. True, except for those signals which have been specifically requested in pre-game instructions by the referee, signals employed by linesmen should be restricted to those that have been approved by the International Football Association Board. Furthermore, such signals should be given in a clear, prompt and decisive manner. Still, without any doubt, the most important consideration by the assessor is whether the decision of the linesman to raise his flag or to avoid signalling is correct. More precisely, the assessor's main consideration is whether the opinion given to the referee by the linesmen, with the aid of a flag, is correct.

Other questions to be answered by the assessor in evaluating the signals of a linesman include the following:

- Was the linesman "flag-happy"?
- Was he over-demonstrative, extravagant or gimmicky in signalling?
- Did he look to the referee on every occasion before giving a signal?
- Did he employ signals that merely confused the referee, to the extent of affecting the latter's match control?
- Did he avoid signalling for infringements that were clearly within the immediate view of the referee?
- Did he avoid signalling behind the referee's back?

It will be observed from the aforementioned assessment form that a maximum of 25 percentage points have been awarded to the linesman for making correct decisions on off-side during a match. This is as it should be. After all, as was pointed out in Chapters 3 and 4, the most important task of a neutral linesman is to judge off-side, except in those rare instances where the referee replaces him in this function by sending him to the goal-line to act as a goal judge.

It has been suggested to me that goal-kicks should have a special place on the form, and that a linesman's performance in assisting the referee with this restart should be worth a maximum of 5 percentage points. I have no quarrel with this suggestion, although I do not believe that a linesman's man-management skills are tested as much at goal-kicks as they are at corner-kicks. Perhaps Point (b) under Signals should read "throw-in and goal-kick", or goal-kicks should be subsumed under Point (e), which deals with ball out of play. Then, again, perhaps the administration of goal-kicks by linesmen should be dealt with under Man Management.

4. Man-management (10 points maximum)

This element of referee-linesman co-operation is inextricably linked to the personality of the linesman. Simply stated, a linesman who is intolerant and who does not use common sense in his dealings with people is unlikely to receive co-operation from players who transgress the Laws of the Game. Similarly, a linesman who engages in conversation or argument with players, team officials or spectators before, during or after the game is unlikely to earn the respect of anyone, and no referee would have confidence in a linesman who did not assist him by advising players with regard to encroachment, time-wasting tactics, position of the ball within the corner-quadrant, and so forth. Such a linesman could be a veritable liability to any referee!

The assessor should watch carefully to see how effective a linesman is in ensuring that substitutions are carried out in accordance with Paragraph (5) of Law III, and the manner in which he deals with named substitutes and bench personnel. (This presupposes that there is no fourth official to undertake these tasks). Perhaps it is no accident that the best linesmen carry out their duties as unobtrusively as possible!

5. Overall Co-operation With The Referee (10 points maximum)

This element of referee-linesman co-operation is similar in significance to "Discipline and Control" that appears as an element of match control on the FIFA and CONCACAF Referee Inspector's Report forms. An assessor who is about to prepare his evaluation report on the field performance of a referee invariably begins by asking himself the following question: Did I witness a game in which the referee maintained discipline and control on the field of play? In preparing his report on the performance of a linesman, the assessor should begin by asking himself the following question: Did I witness a game in which overall referee linesman co-operation was at an acceptable level?

If referee-linesman co-operation was at a high level, chances are that the linesmen contributed to it, and each linesman would probably receive a good grade for this element on the linesman assessment form. If co-operation was at an unacceptable level, and it was determined that the referee did all he could to ensure the success of the Third Team, then the assessor would have to focus on the performance of the linesmen. For each linesman, analysis will probably reveal one or all of the following:

That he did not:
- remain alert and dedicated to his duties, but instead became engrossed in the flow of the game
- maintain his proper position, as necessary, on the on-side/off-side line
- position himself sensibly to make sound judgements in carrying out his assigned tasks
- avoid flag movements which could have been mistaken for signals by the referee
- make certain of never signalling too soon in anticipation of the ball crossing the touch-line or the goal-line
- signal for off-side only when the player in an off-side position was interfering with an opponent, or was involved in active play, or was gaining an advantage by being in an off-side position
- follow the instructions of the referee, even though they were at variance with his own personal opinions
- make certain of never overstepping his bounds by taking it upon himself to apply the Advantage Clause
- maintain eye contact constantly with the referee for possible re-positioning at set plays
- recognize and immediately respond to the referee's signals and gestures that conveyed the referee's need for particular or further advice
- watch carefully for "off-the-ball" incidents and draw the referee's attention to serious offences, especially when they occurred behind the referee's back

This list of derelictions of duty by a linesman is by no means exhaustive. More can be gleaned from the check-list for linesmen that is included in Chapter 7. The chart on page 74 describes in percentage terms the assessment ratings that could be used by national associations to measure the overall field performance of a linesman. These ratings allow one to distinguish between linesmen whose performances are adequate or less than adequate to the task, and to choose between those who are merely competent and those with superior skills.

Assessment Ratings
Referee-Linesman Co-operation

1. Excellent   100%
2. Outstanding   90-99%
3. Very Good   80-89%
4. Good   70-79%
5. Adequate   60-69%
6. Fair   50-59%
7. Unsatisfactory   10-49%

Chapter 7

A Check-List For Linesmen

For years, referees have included a review of the criteria outlined on assessment forms as part of their match preparation routine. Such a review, they claim, not only causes one's adrenaline to flow freely; it also serves as a check-list during one's post-game self-analysis. The following is such a check-list for linesmen.

To the extent that it is possible to do so, the questions on the check-list are categorized in accordance with the criteria for assessing linesmen as discussed in the previous chapter. It is very important to note, though, that there is no intention to suggest that the questions posed under each criterion are the only ones which should be considered for self-analysis. Still, one should not be too far off the mark if these questions are used as a starting-point for such analyses.

1. *Personality*
Did I:

- Conscientiously prepare myself, mentally and physically, for my role as a linesman?

- Enter the field of play smartly attired?

- Carry two clean linesmen's flags in my kit rather than depend upon the home club to provide them?

- Have all the normal accessories of a referee in my kit, and was I prepared to take over the match without warning if the referee sustained an injury or became incapacitated?

- Adopt a friendly and co-operative attitude towards my fellow referees at all times?

- Leave the impression that I was proud to be part of the Third Team?

- Play my part in ensuring that the Third Team was seen to be working together throughout the game?

- Assist the referee to approach the game calmly and confidently?

- Leave the dressing room together with my fellow officials, and accompany them in a smart and confident manner to the centre-circle as a proud member of a match control team?

- Check my flag to ensure that it was securely attached to the flagstick?
- Maintain a high degree of concentration at all times?
- Remain alert and dedicated to my duties rather than become engrossed in the flow of the game?
- Approach my task with confidence, and maintain my composure under pressure?
- Avoid adopting attitudes that made me appear theatrical or arrogant?
- Avoid drawing attention to myself unnecessarily?
- Do all in my power to appear neutral to both teams involved in the match?

2. *Fitness, Mobility, Positioning*
Did I:

- Maintain maximum physical activity for the whole of the game?
- Move nimbly along the touch-lines and goal-lines, and sprint whenever the occasion demanded?
- Follow the ball to the goal-line on all occasions, and was I always in a good position to judge whether the ball had wholly crossed the goal-line?
- Move quickly to the goal-line to act as a goal judge whenever I received a signal from the referee to do so?
- Maintain my proper position, as necessary, on the on-side/off-side line?
- Ensure that I never left my position on the on-side/off-side line at any time to move to the goal-line without an indication from the referee to do so?
- Position myself correctly every time at corner-kicks, goal-kicks and penalty-kicks?
- Position myself sensibly to make sound judgements in carrying out my assigned tasks?
- Avoid running on the touch-line, and thus reduce the chances of damaging the line?
- Conduct a thorough examination of the touch-line and the goal-line that I had to patrol so that I would avoid dips, hollows or obstructions which might have caused me to fall?

3. *Signals*
Did I:

- Carry my flag unfurled, fully downward and in his full view, when I had no advice to give to the referee?

- Face the field of play every time when signalling?

- Change the flag from one hand to another, as necessary, throughout the game to avoid cross-body signaling?

- Look to the referee on every occasion before giving him a flag signal, apart from those instances where it was necessary for me to give a quick signal to indicate that the ball had gone out of play?

- Ensure that I was never "flag-happy", and that I was neither over-demonstrative, extravagant nor gimmicky in signalling?

- Avoid flag movements which could have been mistaken by the referee for signals? For example, did I avoid carrying the flag above waist-level while patrolling the touch-lines and goal-lines?

- Give clear signals as approved by the International Football Association Board, and only the "silent" signals that the referee had asked me to give to him in certain situations?

- Avoid employing other signals that merely confused the referee?

- Avoid using unnecessary signals, including "free hand" signals?

- Make certain that I never signalled too soon at any time because I anticipated that the ball would cross the touch-line or the goal-line?

- Avoid signalling in off-side situations whenever I was in doubt?

- Retain my flag signal whenever it was necessary to do so?

- Make certain that I did not become upset when the referee overruled me, but instead immediately lowered my flag to the downward position and got on with the game?

- Appreciate at all times that my flag signals were not official recognition of the matters signalled, but rather opinions expressed by me to the referee?

- Point my flag at a 45-degree angle in the direction throw-ins were to be taken immediately the ball crossed the touch-line?

- Avoid signalling for infringements that were clearly within the immediate view of the referee?

- Avoid giving signals behind the referee's back?

- Signal for infractions whenever I felt that the referee had not seen them, but that he would have wanted me to signal for them?

- Signal to the referee whenever it was necessary to draw his attention to the other linesman's flag?

- Signal for off-side only when the player in an off-side position was interfering with play or with an opponent, or was gaining an advantage by being in that position, and not simply every time a player was standing in an off-side position?

- Move quickly towards the halfway-line whenever a valid goal was scored, and did I watch for incidents while doing so?

- Remain stationary and await possible consultation with the referee when ever I felt that a goal should not be allowed?

4. *Man-management*
Did I:

- Manage to carry out my assignments effectively by earning the respect and co-operation of the players and team officials?

- Assist the referee by advising players with regard to encroachment, time-wasting tactics, position of the ball within the corner-quadrant, and throw-in and free-kick positions?

- Keep the touch-line that I was patrolling clear of bench personnel, and take proper and sensible action when they encroached?

- Display effective man-management skills, including tolerance, in all my dealings with substitutes and bench personnel?

- Avoid engaging in conversation or argument with players, team officials or spectators before, during and after the garne?

5. *Overall Co-operation With The Referee*
Did I:

- Check the field dimensions and the appurtenances of the game with the referee?

- Check the players' equipment and report to the referee where such equipment was dangerous to another player?

- Check team colors, including those of the goalkeepers, and report to the referee all irregularities with the rules of the competition?

- Listen attentively during the referee's pre-game instructions?

- Follow the instructions of the referee, even though they were at variance with my personal opinions?

- Ask the referee in a polite manner to clarify any uncertainty that arose during his pre-game instructions?

- Ensure that I did not cause the referee to start the game at a later time than was scheduled?

- Carry out all duties that I was asked to perform before the opening kick-off, including inspection of the goal nets?

- Make certain that I never overstepped my bounds at any time by taking upon myself to apply the Advantage Clause?

- Maintain eye contact constantly with the referee for possible re-positioning at set plays?

- Recognize and immediately respond to the referee's signals and gestures that conveyed his need for particular or further advice?

- Watch carefully for "off-the-ball" incidents and draw the referee's attention to serious offences?

- Advise the referee during the half-time interval of "off-the-ball" friction between players which he might not have seen?

- Clarify in the privacy of half-time or post-game discussions any misunderstandings, confusions or breakdown in teamwork in which I was involved during the game?

- Record the names, initials and club identity of players and team officials about whom I will be required as a witness to submit a misconduct report?

- Assist the referee in every possible way before, during and after the game, and did I do so without being unnecessarily intrusive?

- Remember at all times that my job was not to enforce the Laws of the Game, but to assist the referee in his enforcement of them?

If, in self-analysis, a linesman is able to answer each of the foregoing questions in the positive, then he would probably have done all that was expected of him by the referee.

Chapter 8
Practical Drills
for Linesmen

Introduction

The success of the Diagonal System of Match Control is very much dependent upon the movement and positioning of the referee and his two linesmen, as well as the communication between the three. Signals make up the language of this communication, and, as we know, the linesman communicates with the referee by signalling mainly with a flag on a stick.

Throughout a match, linesmen are often required to change the flagstick from one hand to another to avoid cross-body signalling, as well as to ensure that the flag is always in full view of the referee. They are also required to run forward, backward and laterally (side step) with the flagstick in hand. To improve your performance as a linesman, you may find the following drills helpful.

*The author with General Farouk Bouzo, Member of the FIFA Referees'
Committee, at an international referees' symposium in Montreal in April
1994, during which some of the practical drills for linesmen that are
described in this chapter were introduced.*

Drills

Drill #1

Hold the flagstick firmly in one hand, flag unfurled, at your side, and pointing fully downward. While looking directly in front of you, that is, as though facing the field of play, change the flagstick from one hand to another, slowly at first, and then more quickly as you get a feel for the flagstick in your palms. Continue this exercise until you feel very comfortable with this hand-to-hand movement of the flagstick. (For those wishing to check their mechanics, try this drill in front of a mirror). This is a simple exercise to improve your flag-handling skills.

Drill #2

With the flagstick held in your left hand and pointing fully downward at your side as in Drill # 1, run forward as though you are moving along the touch-line toward the corner-flagpost, all the time looking to your left into an imaginary field of play. Simulating game conditions, stop on a dime, make a quick 180 degree-turn while changing the flagstick to the right hand, and run forward as though you are moving along the touch-line toward the half-way line. This time, however, look to your right as you run. Repeat this exercise several times, slowly at first, and more quickly as you get accustomed to all the movements associated with this drill.

Drill #3

With the flagstick held in either hand, flag unfurled, at your side and pointing fully downward, stand with bended knees in a crouch. While looking directly in front of you, take two or three quick side-steps to your right. Stop, and immediately take two or three quick side-steps to your left. Repeat this exercise several times. This is the type of quick lateral movement that a linesman often has to go through in a match in order to maintain a proper position on the on-side/off-side line when there is frantic action between opponents in and around the defending team's penalty-area. In the circumstances, it is not necessary for you to change the flagstick from one hand to the other, lest you drop it!

Drill #4

With the flagstick in your left hand, take three or four quick steps backward and then the same number of steps forward, all the while moving to your right. As you do so, look downward as if you are watching opposing players who are challenging for the ball directly in front of you. Stop, and go through the same manoeuvres while moving to your left, but with the flagstick held in your right hand. Repeat this exercise several times. This drill simulates the movement of a linesman stepping away from the touch-line so as not to impede players who are challenging for the ball in the vicinity.

Referees who make their whistles "talk" are often considered decisive by players, team officials and spectators. Linesmen, on the other hand, are considered decisive when they are resolute in signalling, and especially if they are able to snap their flags while doing so. Flag snapping requires quick wrist action. In other words, "it is a flick of the wrist!"

The following are some useful flag-snapping drills.

Drill #5
Hold the flagstick in one hand, flag unfurled, at your side, and pointing fully downward. While looking in front of you, and as if looking at the referee, snap your flag as you raise the flagstick vertically and to its fullest extent. This is, of course, the basic signal of the linesman. Refer to Figure 2. Lower the flagstick crisply to your side. Repeat this exercise several times, alternating between either hand in holding the flagstick.

Drill #6
Repeat Drill #5. Now, assume that you have to indicate that a player is off-side. Therefore, instead of lowering the flagstick to your side, wait momentarily before lowering it at full arm's length. (Remember that when a linesman raises his flag to signal to the referee that a player is off-side, the flag should not be lowered to indicate where the offence occurred until the referee has acknowledged the signal). Point the flag crisply across an imaginary field of play to indicate in which of three locations the offence occurred, that is, off-side on the far side of the field, or near the centre of the field, or on the near side of the field. Refer to Figures 3(a), 3(b) and 3(c).

Drill #7
Repeat Drill #6. Now, assume that you have to indicate the direction of a throw-in. Instead of lowering the flagstick to your side, lower it so that it is held at a 45-degree angle above the horizontal toward an imaginary goal which is to be attacked. See Figure 6. 1f, during this drill, the flagstick is being held in the right hand in the first instance, but you wish to give a directional signal to your left, it will be necessary for you to change the flagstick to the left hand to avoid cross-body signalling. To do this, lower the flagstick in one smooth action and at an angle, until it is transferred to your left hand in front of you. Continuing this smooth action, raise the flagstick with your left hand and hold it at a 45-degree angle above the horizontal toward the imaginary goal which is to be attacked. Repeat this exercise several times, giving the directional throw-in signal, first to your right, then to your left, and back again to your right

Drill #8
With the flagstick held firmly in the left hand, flag unfurled, and at your side,

sprint forward as though you are moving towards a corner-flagpost, all the time pretending that you are watching a ball that is travelling toward a defending team's goal-line. After sprinting for approximately twenty yards, raise your flagstick crisply (the basic signal of the linesman), as though indicating that the ball has gone out of play beyond the goal-line. Continue running for another six to ten yards, and then point to an imaginary corner-quadrant as if to indicate that a corner-kick is to be awarded (Figure 5), all the time glancing into the field of play, pretending to look at the referee.

Drill #9

Repeat Drill #8. However, after raising your flagstick to indicate that the ball has gone out of play beyond the goal-line, stop, then turn as though to face the field of play. Lower the flagstick and point it horizontally across the field towards an imaginary goal-area to signal that play should be restarted with a goal-kick. See Figure 4.

Drill #10

With the flagstick held in your left hand, start running forward as if moving along a touch-line toward a corner-flagpost, all the time pretending that you are watching a promising goal-attack. Stop, turn around quickly, and switch the flagstick to your right hand. While looking to your right, sprint forward as if moving toward a halfway-line, holding the flagstick at a 45-degree angle below the horizontal and in advance. The latter part of the foregoing simulates the movement by a linesman to inform the referee that a goal has been scored.

Drill #11

Repeat Drill #10, moving laterally (side-stepping) to your right instead of running forward toward an imaginary corner-flagpost.

Drill #12

Starting with the flagstick held in either hand, run up and down an imaginary touch line, slowly at first, changing the flagstick from one hand to another, as necessary. At the same time, repeat Drills #6, 7, 8 and 9, that is, off-side, throw-in, corner-kick and goal-kick, respectively. Repeat these drills in random order. Snap your flag whenever you have to raise it, and lower it crisply. Attempt the exercise while running at different speeds. Occasionally, stop and run laterally as in Drill #3, and backward and forward as in Drill #4. At all times when not signalling, ensure that the flagstick is held below waist-level. Finally, introduce Drills #10 and 11 in the exercise.

Here are three drills that may be quite useful in helping you to improve your ability to concentrate on the movement of players, and especially of those along the on-side/off-side line.

Drill #13

Two officials - a referee and a linesman - are required for this drill which is conducted over one-half of the field of play. The referee is on the field, running along a diagonal, AB, as in Diagram 1 in Chapter 3, with the linesman patrolling the appropriate half of the touch-line. The referee, who is in charge of the drill and whose movements dictate those of the linesman, jogs, walks, sprints, stops, runs forward, backward and laterally, and generally employs at varying speeds any combination of the foregoing movements in an attempt to simulate those of a referee during a match. The linesman is required to imitate the movements of the referee and to do so as quickly as possible without anticipating them.

Drill #14

Two linesmen, facing each other and standing a couple of meters apart, take turns in leading this drill. One linesman begins a series of movements (for example, jumping, side-stepping, squatting, arm raising and body twisting), and the other mimics his actions. The intent of the drill is to have the mimicking linesman concentrate on the actions of his colleague.

Drill #15

At least six people - two in the role of defenders, two as attackers, one as a referee, and one as a linesman - are required for this drill. A ball is also needed. The drill, which may be called "hand soccer", should be conducted over a relatively small area, say, the penalty-area. The attackers throw ("pass") the ball to each other, and the defenders attempt to intercept the "pass." The referee positions himself so that the defenders and attackers are between him and the linesman, with the latter staying at all times in line with the second last defender (or both defenders, if they are level with each other). As soon as the linesman determines that an attacker is off-side, he raises his flag, the referee blows his whistle, and the attackers and defenders switch roles. The "passes" should be made as quickly as possible to cause quick movements by all involved in the drill, and especially by the linesman who must concentrate on the on-side/off-side line. Occasionally, the linesman should also change position with the others so that everyone will have a chance to act as a linesman.

The next two drills are designed to assist the linesman in learning how to maintain eye contact with the referee at all times.

Drill #16

Three people and a ball are required for this drill, which is a variant of Drill #13. The referee runs along a diagonal, with the linesman patrolling the appropriate half of the touch-line. Once again, the referee goes through a series of movements, and the linesman, with flag in hand, imitates these movements.

Occasionally, the third person rolls the ball in a particular direction. The referee moves towards the ball or gets around it, trying to keep the linesman in view as much as possible. In other words, the referee tries to position himself so that the ball is between him and the linesman. For his part, the linesman moves with the referee and maintains eye contact with him while keeping an eye on the ball. The three people involved in the drill should switch roles occasionally.

Drill #17

Just a referee and a linesman are required for this drill. The linesman leads the drill, jogging, sprinting, walking, stopping, etc., and the referee copies these actions. Occasionally, and while maintaining eye contact with the referee, the linesman signals for different stoppages in play, and the referee reacts accordingly. The referee should sometimes anticipate the linesman's signal, and award, say, a goal-kick instead of a corner-kick. In the circumstances, the linesman quickly lowers his flag and gets on the same wave-length as the referee.

FIFA's Physical Fitness Tests

The foregoing drills are by no means arduous. In fact, if you are capable of passing FIFA's physical fitness tests for international linesmen, you should easily complete the entire set of drills in less than one hour.

The physical fitness tests for linesmen are described below.

For Linesmen:

- 50-metre sprint within a maximum of 7.5 seconds (1st time)
- 50-metre sprint within a maximum of 7.5 seconds (2nd time)
- 12-minute run, minimum distance of 2,700 meters
  - walking not permitted

The times and the distances indicated above are the minimum criteria that are applied by FIFA and most national associations in testing the physical fitness of linesmen. Some national associations go further in requiring all their match officials to pass FIFA's physical fitness tests for international referees. That makes sense, bearing in mind that linesmen are sometimes required to take over the match without warning if the referee sustains an injury or becomes incapacitated. The times and the distances of the physical fitness tests for referees are described below.

For Referees:

- 50-metre sprint within a maximum of 7.5 seconds (1st time)

- 200-metre sprint within a maximum of 32 seconds (1st time)
- 50-metre sprint within a maximum of 7.5 seconds (2nd time)
- 200-metre sprint within a maximum of 32 seconds (2nd time)
- 12-minute run, minimum distance of 2,700 meters
  - walking not permitted

Epilogue

For certain, some soccer fans around the world had their knives sharpened long before the opening game of the 1994 World Cup in Chicago's Soldier Field. They were waiting anxiously, preparing to pounce upon FIFA if its policy of using specialist linesmen in the games were to fail.

Failure would bring cries of "I told you so!", even though, following dreadful displays of linesmanship in the previous three or four World Cups, just about everyone was of the opinion that it would be infinitely better for FIFA to use specialists on the lines than to have international referees performing as linesmen in major tournaments.

Thankfully, these fans never had the opportunity to use their knives, for the officiating in the 1994 World Cup was arguably the best that one has ever seen in the history of the competition.

No player got away with "Hand of God" offences, referees dutifully followed explicit instructions to deal severely with violent tackles from behind, cynical fouls were discouraged from the outset, injured players were hastily and sometimes literally carted off the pitch in an effort to increase playing time, and considerably more referees displayed acceptable levels of physical fitness in the scorching heat and high humidity of American cities than they had done in previous World Cups. Furthermore, overall referee-linesman co-operation was of a relatively high order.

Oh, there were a few linesmen who did not always approach their task with confidence. Two or three were clearly ponderous in their movements along the touch-line, the odd one lacked flag-handling dexterity, some failed to always maintain their proper position on the on-side/off-side line, and one or two, who apparently believe there is a new Off-side Law (what with all the talk about "active and passive off-side" and "area of active play"), appeared at times to be utterly confused when they had to judge off-side situations.

But, as a group, the linesmen in the 1994 World Cup performed satisfactorily, in the sense that they enhanced the performances of the referees (or, at least, they did not hamper them!)

Having said that, it is well to remind referees once more that it is imperative for them to recognize that linesmen are not just an adjunct to the game, but that they are a very important part of it.

There is no doubt in my mind that linesmanship all over the world will get better, and that this will occur at a very rapid pace as a result of improved training and a greater desire by linesmen to accept more appointments for duty on the line than as referees "in the middle." The pride and status of linesmen should also improve with increased acceptance of their performances by referees.

For their part, as they receive more and more appointments, and preferably for the major FIFA tournaments, international linesmen will become increasingly more confident, with the result that it shall not be long before their skill levels are on a par with those of the referees in the Final Tournament of World Cup Competitions. Then, and only then, will soccer fans concentrate on the virtuosity of the star players of the sport, and leave dissection of the performances of match officials to administrators, instructors, assessors, and fellow referees and linesmen. At least, we can only hope so!

Bibliography

1. CARON, Guy and Pierre SCHWINTE, **EL ARBITRAJE DEL FUTBOL**, Hispano Europea, Barcelona, 1982.

2. CONCACAF, **GUIA DEL ARBITRO**, Guatemala, 1986.

3. EVANS, Robert, **MANUAL FOR LINESMEN**, North Texas Soccer Referees' Association, Dallas, 1973.

4. FIFA, **LAWS OF THE GAME**, Zurich, 1995 Annual Edition, (English, French, Spanish and German).

5. ____, **NOTES: Seminar For Referees And Linesmen, 14-18 March, 1994, Dallas**, Zurich, 1994.

6. HARRIS Jr., Paul E. and Larry R. HARRIS, **FAIR OR FOUL?**, California, 1973; revised in 1975 and 1978.

7. HOWELL, Denis, **SOCCER REFEREEING**, Pelham Books, London, August,1968.

8. LOVER, Stanley, **ASSOCIATION FOOTBALL MATCH CONTROL**, Pelham Books, London, 1970.

9. MATHURIN, D.C. Emerson, **A PRIMER FOR INSTRUCTORS OF BEGINNING SOCCER REFEREES**, The Canadian Soccer Association, Ottawa, 1991, Third Edition.

10. ____, **IN SEARCH OF FAIR PLAY,** ONEREAL, Ottawa, 1993, Second Edition.

11. RING, Ted, **THE ASSESSOR'S CHALLENGE: A Comprehensive Guide For Association Football Referee Assessors**, The Referees' Association, Coventry, 1994.

12. ROUS, Sir Stanley and Donald FORD, **A HISTORY OF THE LAWS OF ASSOCIATION FOOTBALL**, FIFA, Zurich, 1974.

13. SELLIN, Eric, **THE INNER GAME OF SOCCER**, World Publications, California, 1976.

14. TAYLOR, Jack, **SOCCER REFEREEING**, Faber and Faber, London, 1978.

15. THE FOOTBALL ASSOCIATION, **HANDBOOK FOR REFEREE ASSESSORS**, London, January, 1994.

16. ____, **THE FA GUIDE FOR REFEREES AND LINESMEN**, London, 1974.

17. THE REFEREES' ASSOCIATION, **MANUAL OF GUIDANCE FOR REFEREES**, Coventry, 1994.

18. UNITED STATES SOCCER FEDERATION, **PROCEDURES FOR REFEREES, LINESMEN AND FOURTH OFFICIALS**, Chicago, 1994.

19. YAMASAKI, Arturo Maldonado, **REGLAS DEL FUTBOL ILLUSTRADAS**, Mexico, 1973.

Films

1. FA Films on **REFEREEING**, in colour; a series of four instructional films, 25 minutes each
   Film 1: **Managing Set Plays**
   Film 2: **Positioning and Movement**
   Film 3: **Fair and Unfair Challenges**
   Film 4: **Dealing with Unsporting Behavior**

2. FA, **JUDGING CHALLENGES**; in color, 29 minutes.

3. FIFA, **REFEREE AND LINESMEN - a Team**; an instructional film; in color, 21 minutes.

4. FIFA, **THE REFEREE IN ACTION**, based on incidents from the 1990 World Cup in Italy; in colour, 42 minutes.

5. FIFA, **REFEREES' INSTRUCTIONS**; based on incidents from the 1986 World Cup in Mexico; in colour, 22 minutes.

6. FIFA, **LAW XII: TOWARDS UNIFORMITY OF INTERPRETATION**, based on incidents from the 1970 World Cup in Mexico; in colour, 25 minutes.

7. UNITED STATES SOCCER FEDERATION, **LAW XI: OFFSIDE**; based on incidents from the 1994 World Cup in the United States; in co-operation with FIFA; in color, 25 minutes.

8. UNITED STATES SOCCER FEDERATION, **DEALING WITH FOUL PLAY**; based on incidents from the 1994 World Cup in the United States; in co-operation with FIFA; in color, 20 minutes.

9. VIRGIN VISION, **FOUL PLAY**; in color, 55 minutes.

NOTES

Published by **REEDSWAIN Videos and Books**
612 Pughtown Road
Spring City, Pennsylvania 19475, USA
1-800-331-5191 • www.reedswain.com

NOTES

Published by **REEDSWAIN Videos and Books**
612 Pughtown Road
Spring City, Pennsylvania 19475, USA
1-800-331-5191 • www.reedswain.com

NOTES

Published by **REEDSWAIN Videos and Books**
612 Pughtown Road
Spring City, Pennsylvania 19475, USA
1-800-331-5191 • www.reedswain.com

NOTES

Published by **REEDSWAIN Videos and Books**
612 Pughtown Road
Spring City, Pennsylvania 19475, USA
1-800-331-5191 • www.reedswain.com